The Sleeping Bea...

THE SLEEPING BEAUTY SYNDROME

Jean Freeman

sheldon **PRESS**

First published in Great Britain in 1993
Sheldon Press, SPCK, Marylebone Road, London NW1 4DU

© Jean Freeman 1993

British Library Cataloguing-in-Publication Data
A catalogue record for this book is available from the
British Library

ISBN 0–85969–641–3

Photoset by Deltatype Ltd, Ellesmere Port, Cheshire
Printed in Great Britain by Biddles Ltd, Guildford and
King's Lynn

Contents

Introduction

Once upon a time, there was a king and queen who longed for a child. Then, after years of waiting, the queen found she was going to have a baby. They were so overjoyed when their daughter was born that they arranged a large Christening. Among the guests were twelve fairies, who wished on the baby princess gifts of happiness, beauty, health, contentment, wisdom and goodness.

But just as the twelfth fairy was about to make her wish, the castle doors flew open and in swept the thirteenth fairy, a bad, evil fairy, who was furious that she had not been invited to the christening. Waving her wand over the baby's cradle, she cast a spell, not a wish. 'On her sixteenth birthday,' she hissed, 'the princess will prick herself with a spindle. And she will die.'

A terrible hush fell over the party. Then the twelfth fairy stepped forward. She had been about to wish the gift of joy on the baby, but now she had to try and prevent the princess's death. 'My magic is not strong enough to break the wicked spell,' she said, 'but instead of dying, the princess will fall asleep for a hundred years.'

The princess grew into the happiest, kindest and most beautiful child anyone had ever seen. All the wishes of the eleven fairies had come true. The king banned all the spindles from his kingdom to prevent the wicked fairy's spell from working. But just before her sixteenth birthday, the princess decided to explore parts of the castle where she had been forbidden to go when she was a child. She climbed a spiral staircase to a turret and opened a door into a little room where an old woman, dressed in black, sat spinning. 'What are you doing?' the princess asked, as she had never seen anything like it in her life.

'Come and see, pretty girl', replied the old lady. The princess watched fascinated as, deftly, she pulled strands of wool from some sheep's fleece and fed it into the spindle.

'Would you like to try?' the old woman asked cunningly.

In a flash, the princess had pricked her finger on the spindle. With blood on her finger, she fell to the floor, as if dead.

But the twelfth fairy's wish had worked. The princess did not die, but fell into a deep sleep. And the spell worked on everyone in the castle as well. The king and queen fell asleep, as did all their guests and servants. In the kitchen, the cook fell asleep as she was about to box the pot boy's ears, and the scullery maid nodded off as she plucked a chicken. A great silence descended on the castle.

As the years passed, a thorn hedge grew up around the castle. Several suitors, hearing the story of the beautiful, sleeping princess, tried to fight their way through the thorns. But none was able to reach her.

One day, a hundred years later, a handsome prince rode by. He stopped to ask an old woodsman what lay behind the tall, thick thorn hedge. When he heard about Sleeping Beauty, he got out his sword and cut through the hedge until he reached the castle, where he found everyone asleep. Finally, he reached the little room in the turret and gazed down at the most beautiful girl he had ever seen. Without hesitating, he leaned over her and gently kissed her.

As his lips touched hers, the princess opened her eyes. She gazed into the prince's eyes and instantly fell in love.

Meanwhile, in the great hall, the king and queen were stretching and yawning and wondering how they could have dropped off to sleep in the middle of the day. In the kitchen, the cook boxed the pot boy's ears and the scullery maid continued plucking the chicken.

The one hundred years spell had been broken and the prince and princess were married. After the wedding, they rode off together to their new home in the prince's kingdom, where they lived happily ever after.

1
Falling in Love – From Fantasy to Reality

On the surface, Sleeping Beauty seems a romantic little tale. There's the beautiful heroine, waiting for her prince to come along, while all her other suitors, the ones who can't fight through the thorn hedge around her castle, fail to win her heart. Even the pricking of Sleeping Beauty's finger, which sends her into a deep sleep, can be seen as a delaying tactic along the path of true love, just as other heroines usually have to overcome an obstacle or two along the way before they end up with their Mr Right.

But Sleeping Beauty, like every woman, has hidden depths.

Fairy tales have kept their appeal throughout the centuries because they illustrate the complexities of human relationships. Every character represents emotions that we have all felt at one time or another in our lives. Envy, anger, guilt, fear, rejection and loss are all featured in these extraordinary little tales, along with sibling rivalry, jealous mothers and fathers who have favourite children or who don't want their daughters to grow up.

These characters show us feelings that, whatever age we are, we need to master if we are to relate to others in a livelier and more satisfying way. Each fairy story provides us with a psychological map, which can help us find our way to achieving more fulfilling relationships. Their message is that human relationships are a struggle, but we can overcome our difficulties, if, like the hero or heroine in these stories, we are prepared to take on the challenge.

The Sleeping Beauty is a tale about a girl growing up into a woman, mature enough to have a fulfilling relationship with a man. Along the way are the obstacles that she first has to overcome before she can break away from her childhood dependence on her parents and find her adult self. The problems she faces are typical of any teenager. She has to struggle with her parents' reluctance to let her grow up, illustrated in the tale by the king and queen trying to prevent Sleeping Beauty pricking her finger on the 'wicked' fairy's spinning wheel, which symbolizes her growing up.

But it is when the princess falls asleep to inwardly prepare for this transformation into a woman that she faces her biggest challenge. Her temptation is to 'stay asleep', or, in other words, to remain unchanged from being her parents' beautiful, special little daughter, instead of waking up to the harder, but more rewarding task of discovering her own identity. It is the same temptation that every young girl has to overcome if she is to become emotionally mature. It is also the same temptation every woman faces when she has an intimate, sexual relationship. Each time she falls in love, she has the choice of remaining the same person or allowing herself to grow emotionally and discover real meaning in her relationships.

Sleeping Beauty is represented as a young girl, but that does not mean that growing up emotionally is something that happens automatically on the eve of our eighteenth birthday. It is a process that we need to continue throughout our lives if we are to understand ourselves better and have the kind of relationships we want. Every significant relationship in our adult lives offers us the chance of gaining more emotional maturity and a more fulfilling way of relating to the men we love.

The Sleeping Beauty Syndrome is about the process of growing up, which means continuing the struggle to understand ourselves better so we can find what we really want from life, no matter what age we happen to be. A woman can be caught in the Sleeping Beauty Syndrome even though her life is successful in other ways. She may have a good career, have a live-in lover, be a wife and mother, yet she still has not achieved a really close and satisfying partnership. When it comes to her relationships, she has never really achieved emotional maturity.

The Sleeping Beauty woman often finds that she chooses the 'wrong' man, makes the same mistakes or never achieves real intimacy in her relationships. In psychological terms, what she is likely to be doing is repeating patterns of relating learnt in childhood, when as a child she had to live up to an image of herself instead of becoming the person she was meant to be. Like Sleeping Beauty, a part of herself is still sleeping; she has never discovered her real identity, which means she still cannot find what she wants from her life.

Childhood is not the idyllic state our parents may have tried to pretend it was or that we like to remember it as being. It is not a separate, disconnected state that we leave behind us when we grow up. It contains the pleasures and pain, the joy and sadness that are part and parcel of human existence. The way we learn to cope with the powerful feelings involved in our childhood relationships has a profound effect on the rest of our lives.

The difference between childhood and adult life is that a child is experiencing relationships for the first time. She has no prior knowledge and no real sense of her own identity to help her understand and cope with the conflicting feelings that she discovers in herself and in her relationship with her family. Many of these feelings are connected with the frustrations and disappointments that seem so overwhelming in childhood, with the ensuing rage of being such a powerless, little person, who is so dependent on her parents. But feeling anger and resentment towards the two people she loves most in the world causes great conflict in a child who is too immature to know such feelings are not wrong or bad. What she wants is her parents to help her to understand herself and the way she feels. But parents, often with the best intentions, may not want to recognize their child's emotional conflicts. They want her to be happy, so they try and protect her from feelings that might cause conflict in their family life. They don't want to face feelings their child has that might also stir up vulnerable feelings in themselves. A little girl wants to be the daughter her parents can love, so she represses the aspects of herself that don't fit the image of a pleasing, compliant child. She begins to grow up into someone who is cut off from her individuality.

Fairy tales tell a different story. They show children and adults alike that what we really feel isn't unique or wrong. In a simple, straightforward language, they identify feelings we all experience in our relationships and makes sense of them in a much more realistic way. And, like the child we once were, we still listen to these stories because they echo our own inner experience.

The Sleeping Beauty woman has not yet found her real self. It has remained asleep since childhood, when she became the child her parents wanted, not the person she was meant to be. This is what holds her back from achieving a mature and loving relationship in her adult life. What she still can't let go is her childhood fear that she won't be loved if she becomes herself.

Secretly, she may be still hanging onto her childhood fantasy of waiting for her 'prince', the 'right' man, to come along. But by hanging onto her illusions, she is danger of sleeping her life away.

Every relationship does offer us the possibility of transforming our lives, but not in a magical way. That transformation happens if we treat a relationship as part of a continuing process of self discovery that leads towards greater maturity. An intimate, sexual relationship connects us with our real feelings, which in other, less intense situations, we often hide, even from ourselves. By becoming emotionally vulnerable in a relationship we can learn to understand ourselves and the way we relate to others. Each time we fall in love, we can simply plunge into a relationship, hoping that we will be lucky this time and have finally found the right man. Or we can see it as a chance to create a relationship that gives more meaning to our lives.

The Sleeping Beauty is a tale about a girl growing up into a woman, mature enough to have a fulfilling relationship with a man. Along the way are the obstacles that she first has to overcome before she can break away from her childhood dependence on her parents and find her adult self.

One of her problems is that she is 'blessed' with being the happiest, kindest, most beautiful child anyone has ever seen. She is a 'perfect' child, the kind of daughter that every parent wants. If it wasn't for the arrival of the 'wicked' fairy, she might never have really grown up. She would have gone on playing the part of her parents' lovable little girl all her life.

The thirteenth fairy's 'curse' that the princess will prick her finger on a spindle and then fall asleep represents the awakening of her sexuality. The drawing of blood indicates the start of menstruation, the sign that she has grown up physically. But because this fairy was the uninvited guest, the one that the princess's parents didn't want at her christening, she also symbolizes the princess's emerging, grown-up feelings. These feelings are disturbing, not because they are bad or wicked, but because they make the princess different from the little girl she once was. They disturb the image her parents want to keep of their daughter.

In recognizing that she has different feelings from her parents, the princess begins to wake up to the fact that she is also different from the perfect daughter she had been expected to be. She has begun to recognize herself as a person with her own emerging identity.

But separating ourselves from our parents' expectations is a hard struggle. It is part of a process that continues throughout our lives. And as the fairy story shows, before she is able to do that, the princess has to fall asleep. Before any major transition in life, we often withdrew into ourselves to sort out the conflicting feelings about what we will lose and gain from this change in ourselves. It is a period of inner preparation from which Sleeping Beauty emerged with a sufficient sense of her own adult identity to be ready for a sexual relationship, symbolized as an awakening by her prince.

The fairy tale also warns of the dangers of a sleep that lasts too long. Sleeping Beauty's temptation is to remain exactly as she was – her parents' perfect, little daughter. The story shows how, as she sleeps, she stays beautiful and youthful, unchanged because she has no experience that would have enabled her to mature into a woman. Everyone around her falls asleep too, which represents the self-absorption and isolation of a young girl's 'sleep'. The world, as she sees it, remains as it appeared in her 'idyllic' childhood. There is no suffering or pain, but no knowledge or experience to be gained either.

It is the same world the Sleeping Beauty woman gets caught in, unless she realizes her need to change the image she has of herself.

The Sleeping Beauty woman may yearn for more intimacy with her partner, more challenge in her work, more closeness in her family life. But however hard she tries to find what she is looking for, it still eludes her. Changing partners, getting a different job or moving house doesn't transform her life in the way she wants. Outward changes don't have a lasting effect until she wakes up to the need to change inwardly first.

She has to let go of being the daughter her parents wanted to become a woman who knows she can be loved for her real self. What a child wants is to feel loved. So she represses feelings that make her parents appear to withdrew or turn away from her. She learns to protect herself from the hurt and humiliation of having her most sensitive feelings misunderstood or ignored. But each time that happens, she loses touch with a little bit of her own identity. Instead of childhood being a time of self-discovery, she starts building layers of protection around herself. She becomes like Sleeping Beauty, who slept with thorn bushes surrounding her castle so no one could reach her real self.

A woman expresses her own adult identity through establishing herself in her own career, by having sexual relationships and her own life-style. But if she has not acquired an inner connection with her real self, she is likely to depend too much on these relationships for her identity. Without someone or something to make her feel good about herself, she feels empty and worthless inside. Her relationships never seem to give her what she needs because she is still trying to live up to what others want of her, just as she did in childhood. She still has to discover that she can be loved for herself.

Just as she lives up to other people's expectations, she also expects too much of others; so she never feels really contented or satisfied with her life. Each time she feels let down, she imagines that it will be different next time. She is still secretly waiting for the 'right' man, and the 'perfect' relationship that she dreamed of as a child.

A Sleeping Beauty woman can have such an effective camouflage that she is not easy to recognize. In fact, she may be the sort who gets admired and envied for being so apparently mature and able to cope with adult life. She may be intensely ambitious, either for herself or her partner. She appears such a successful career woman, who runs her home and brings up her children so well, that others are always saying what a marvel she is. She works hard at creating a smooth, impenetrable façade.

What she hides is a sense of emptiness, as if nothing she does has any real meaning. Normally, she keeps herself too busy to allow herself to experience such feelings, but when she does she becomes depressed and anxious. She will become moody for no particular reason, except an underlying dissatisfaction with her life.

Usually she says what she feels expected to say, not what she really feels. But, sometimes, the effort of always trying to do the right thing proves too much and then the part of herself which contains her real feelings will burst out in childish rages or tears. 'Pull yourself together', an inner voice tells her. 'Look at all you've got. You've no right to make a fuss.' So she shuts off these disturbing feelings by taking on even more challenges. If only she had a different partner, another job, more money or a nicer house, she imagines she would feel better about herself.

As a child, she remembers how her parents praised her for being so grown up or such a clever girl. She sees the demands they made on her to succeed as their wanting the best for her. She says she was fortunate to have such wonderful parents, who did so much for her. What she has hidden from herself are her real feelings about always needing to strive to win their praise and approval. She has 'forgotten' the fear and loneliness she never openly admitted, which came from constantly trying to live up to their image and the fear of failing them. She still can't take her parents off a pedestal. She keeps them up there as a protection, so she does not have to experience her anger about always having to struggle for their approval – and never quite measuring up.

The Sleeping Beauty woman's image of herself may have grown to fit her so tightly that even she believes it is the real her. It is only occasionally, when she finds herself feeling completely differently from what she expected, that she glimpses there's a different person inside her. This realization may happen when she suddenly says or does something that is completely out of character. She may try to cover it up saying she didn't know what possessed her to behave like that, while, inwardly, she feels excited yet scared by this new-found glimpse of herself. But she is still afraid of her real self being rejected if she doesn't keep control over that part of herself.

Nothing in her life seems to live up to her expectations. She finds herself unable fully to enjoy praise or compliments for what she has achieved. When people congratulate her, it feels as if they are talking about someone she doesn't really know, someone who isn't her, while the achievement itself feels hollow and empty. What she achieves has no meaning for her real self.

Pat, 28, is an actress, who has appeared in small, supporting roles in several TV plays and comedies. But she's never become a respected, 'serious' actress or a star, except in her mother's eyes.

Although Pat loves acting, she has become depressed and dissatisfied about her career. No role seems to excite or interest her. It feels as if she's played the same part over and over again. Even praise for a good performance no longer means much to her. She feels she's just learnt a few acting tricks to fool people into thinking she's a good actress. Inwardly, she knows that she's not putting anything of herself into her parts.

One of Pat's earliest memories is standing in a corner of the lounge at home and reciting nursery rhymes to impress her mother's family and friends. 'You were only two years old – and you had such an amazing memory', her mother still says proudly.

Right from the start, Pat knew 'great' things were expected of her. She was brighter than average, but not the genius her mother imagined. Whatever success she had at school was achieved by hard work, a good memory and fear. Her whole future seemed to depend on passing her exams. 'It upsets your father and me so much when you don't do well,' her mother told her. 'We're depending on you.'

Sometimes the pressure seemed so great that Pat nearly passed out when she turned her exam paper over and saw questions she couldn't answer. But somehow her memory always got her through. Being successful and the centre of attention was the image Pat was always living up to as a child. She showed some acting talent at school and worked hard to get starring roles in school plays. Yet afterwards, she would feel humiliated when she heard her mother boasting in a loud voice about her performance. What she hid inwardly was her resentment and anger about always having to 'perform' to feel she was wanted. But she had so little confidence in her real self that she was afraid of feeling a 'nobody' if she didn't try to please.

Her acting career was an attempt to break free of her parents' expectations. It was also Pat's first attempt to find her real self, but at the same time, she hedged her bets, by choosing a job where she still had to perform and win praise.

What she did was break the mould that her parents were so eager to fit her into, as they set their hearts on her going to university and then settling down in a respectable profession, such as the law or architecture. Acting was a waste of her 'wonderful brain', her mother told her, as well as being totally insecure.

There had never been so many rows at home before. 'You were always such a good child', her mother told her. 'The way you're going on now is making your father ill.' But Pat was determined. Her attempt to break free of her dependence on her parents had stirred up a liveliness and independence in her, so for the first time she began to get a sense of her own selfworth. She was so determined, that rather than lose their daughter, her parents finally gave in.

Pat showed promise at drama school and afterwards, being an attractive, young girl, she didn't find it difficult to get small roles playing glamorous secretaries or sexy barmaids in provincial theatre productions. She developed a nice, light touch for comedy and even managed to land a few TV parts. Soon her photograph was appearing in the local paper in her home town with headlines such as 'Local girl appears on TV'. Pat was back in the role of the family's 'star' performer again.

But the novelty of seeing her name among the long list of

supporting actors in a TV comedy, gradually began to wear thin. Inwardly, Pat was still that little girl standing in the corner of the lounge, reciting nursery rhymes to please her mother. She had never taken roles that challenged her by being outside her normal, acting range because she still had not let go of her childhood image of herself. She was still trying to live up to her parents' expectations, instead of becoming a woman prepared to risk failure in order to gain her own identity and what she wanted from her life.

Another type of Sleeping Beauty woman is the opposite of the high achiever. In fact, she is often afraid of being successful or good at anything other than putting other people's feelings before her own. Her feelings don't count, just as they didn't as a child. What came first in childhood was her parents', and particularly her mother's needs. She quickly learned that her mother easily got upset or had one of her bad headaches if she was difficult or disobedient. So she began to ignore her own feelings and became ultra sensitive to her mother's moods.

At home, she was a 'wonderful' daughter, her mother's 'little treasure'. 'What would I do without you?', her mother often said. It was as if she was the one being mother, not the other way around. But repressing her own feelings meant she lacked any real sense of her own identity, which made her intensely vulnerable to criticism and unable to stand up for herself. She played the role her parents wanted, as she was afraid of feeling the emptiness that was left inside from denying her own feelings. As a child, she may have sensed how envious it might make her mother if, instead of a possession, she became a person in her own right.

This kind of woman continues to live out that childhood image in her adult life. She is shy and highly sensitive towards other people's feelings, but at the same time feels a deep resentment that no one takes the time or trouble to understand the 'real' her. She often withdraws into a world of her own, where she nurses her wounded feelings and secretly feels superior to all those people who have unknowingly hurt or misunderstood her. Outwardly she is terrified of voicing her own opinions or showing strong emotions in case her fragile sense of self-confidence is shattered.

Often this type of woman will hide behind a more outwardly self-assured partner. 'How can she stay with such a bad-tempered, impossible man?' her friends wonder. What keeps her is her partner's ability to express the feelings she's so afraid of voicing herself. But however outwardly different her partner appears, it is also likely that she has picked someone who is all bark and no bite, with a sense of identity as fragile as her own. She clings to him as she once did to her mother, by indulging his moods and putting his feelings first.

Mandy, 25, is the youngest of three daughters. She enjoys her job as a primary school teacher but, compared to the rest of her family, she feels a failure. Both her sisters went to university and now earn big salaries in accountancy and advertising careers.

Mandy's first serious relationship with a man ended when he met someone else. Mandy was very hurt, but not really surprised. She was used to feeling second best.

Right from childhood, Mandy felt she was an unwanted child. Her parents' marriage was in trouble before she was born and if it hadn't been for her unexpected arrival, her mother always says she would have left her father. The fact that her parents remained together didn't relieve Mandy of feeling guilty for 'ruining' her mother's life. 'I missed my chance of getting a divorce by staying to look after you when you were small', her mother explains. 'By the time you'd grown up, I was too old to start a new life.'

As a child, Mandy was always scared when her parents quarrelled. Often, she would hear her mother threatening to pack her bags and walk out. Mandy did not do as well as she could have done at school because she often found it difficult to concentrate. She worried that when she got home her mother would have carried out her threat to leave.

To keep her mother, she was always trying to please. As noise gave her mother a headache, Mandy became a quiet child who rarely brought friends round to the house. She also tried hard to be cheerful, as it upset her mother if she appeared sad. Her mother often talked to her about her marriage problems and Mandy listened, flattered that she was her mother's confidante. It didn't occur to her that her mother never seemed interested in any problems that she had. Inwardly, Mandy felt so confused about her own identity that she clung to her mother. She repressed her own feelings in order to keep her mother's love.

When Mandy grew up, she fell in love with an intellectual, but emotionally withdrawn, man, similar to her father. She was immensely flattered when he became interested in her too, and, at first, Mandy's real self began to blossom in the relationship. She became lively and playful with her lover. She was making up for all the playing she had missed as a child. As she started to 'open up' in the relationship, she began to express feelings and opinions that were her own. But Mandy's sense of her own identity was still fragile and she needed to be constantly reassured that her lover found her attractive to feel good about herself. She was always on the lookout for any signs that might show he had lost interest in her and would go off with someone who was more attractive and intelligent.

Mandy's lack of self-worth, combined with her boyfriend's fear of emotional involvement, were the real causes behind the break up of her first love affair. But, painful though losing her lover had been, her first relationship helped Mandy to start growing up. In her relationship, Mandy had got her a glimpse of herself as a different person from the quiet, well-behaved daughter who put other people's feelings first. The liveliness and spontaneity that she had discovered in herself when the affair began had showed her that she could be a different person from the one she had become.

Losing her mother had been her deepest fear in childhood. Losing her lover meant she had experienced and survived those fears, which gave her the emotional strength to start becoming herself.

'Thank goodness I'm not like my parents. I couldn't be more different.' But becoming the opposite of the kind of daughter her parents wanted does not mean a woman is expressing her adult self. More likely, she is still tied to her parents' expectations by always having to react against them. This Sleeping Beauty woman will choose partners, jobs, often a whole life-style that she knows is bound to anger, upset or disappoint her parents. Inwardly, she is so angry with them, she can't stop punishing them for not accepting and understanding her real self.

On the surface, her rebellion may show itself in little ways. She will vote Labour because her parents were always staunch Tories. She will dress sloppily or inappropriately, simply because her mother never had a hair out of place. She has no time for people who only seem to care about keeping up appearances, as that's what seemed to matter most to her parents when she was growing up. She will pick partners who appear the opposite of her father;

be a liberal, anything-goes mother because her own parents seemed so narrow-minded and strict. She is a person of extremes. There never seems to be a middle road.

As a child, she may have felt suffocated by her parents' over-protectiveness. All they seemed to care about were her achievements, so they could boast about her and the wonderful career that she was bound to have. Or, instead of being the family's pride and joy, she felt the failure, pushed aside by brothers or sisters who fulfilled her parents' expectations in a way she never could. So, she became the family rebel, the anti-hero, who always gave her family something to talk about. If she couldn't be a success in her parents' terms, she would be someone who forced them to notice her in other ways. She had so little sense of her real identity that she constantly needed to be noticed. She got the feeling she didn't exist when she was ignored.

Imogen, 24, had grown up into a young woman who had become a constant disappointment to her parents. Her whole life seemed so far removed from the brilliant future they had imagined for their only daughter, who had once been such a 'model' child.

Her mother remembered fondly how immaculately dressed Imogen had always been as a little girl. She had hated having a spot of dirt on her clothes, yet now she usually looked such a mess. She was so passionately involved in environmental and left-wing political causes that she claimed she could not be bothered with keeping up the kind of appearance that her mother spent her whole life worrying about.

The change in Imogen had happened during her late teens, when she fell in love with a political activist, who had long hair and got arrested on protest demonstrations. She had chucked her chance to go to university and instead had taken a number of jobs that paid the rent on the bedsit she shared with her current boyfriend and gave her time for her political activities.

The first boyfriend had several successors, each one looking just as long-haired, scruffy and far removed from Imogen's parents' idea of a suitable partner for their nicely-brought-up child. Imogen's life-style represented her way of finding her own adult identity, except that it did not give her the satisfaction that she had expected to find. If she was honest with herself, she wasn't nearly as committed to her political causes as her boyfriends. Nor was she as happy with her free-spirited, anti-establishment lovers as she made out. In each affair, she found herself getting irritated with these men for their constant criticism of all those who had 'made it' in a capitalistic society. At times, she even found herself reacting like her mother and wishing that these blokes of hers would stop moaning and get a proper career for themselves.

The one thing that seemed constant in Imogen's life was her anger against her parents for their continuing inability to understand or accept her as she was. Imogen's rebellion against her parents was her way of trying to break free from the constrictions of her childhood and the image she'd had to live up to of an immaculately dressed, spotless little girl.

But her lifestyle was not a real transition into adulthood, but a way of trying to sort out the feelings between herself and her parents that lay under the surface of her relationship with them. Her messy appearance and lifestyle also represented feelings that had been hidden from her parents during her childhood for fear of messing up the 'spotless' image of their family life.

Inwardly, Imogen wanted to achieve more in her life. Her irritation at her boyfriends' attitudes towards conventional careers, also expressed her own frustration about rejecting opportunities that might have led to finding a more satisfying career.

Imogen's parents might never understand their daughter, but what was important was that she began to understand herself. Then she could stop being an ageing adolescent, constantly reacting against what her parents had wanted for her and find what she wanted in her own life.

How much of a Sleeping Beauty woman are you? Ask yourself these questions.

- Are you always driven to achieve more than others? Are you terrified of feeling humiliated if you fail?
- Are you always seeking admiration or approval? Are you afraid you won't be liked if you say what you really feel?
- Do you feel expected to be reliable and sensible? Do you put on a brave face, so no one knows when you're unhappy or sad?
- Do you constantly monitor how others react to you? Do you always put other people's feelings before your own?
- Are you fiercely independent and proud of it? Or do you cling

to relationships that you know aren't what you really want, but you're frightened of letting go?

Think about these questions. Then imagine yourself back in childhood. Are the questions that apply to you now the same ones that you would have answered Yes to when you were a child? Each of these questions is about being trapped in an image of ourselves that goes back to childhood. Inwardly, we are still being driven by the same voice that our parents used, which seemed to be wanting us to be someone other than ourselves.

The Sleeping Beauty woman wants to be loved. She may be loved by her partner and her family, but inwardly she can't believe she really is. 'If they really knew me, they wouldn't love me', she tells herself, because that is how it felt when she was a child. However loving her parents appeared, it always seemed theirs was a conditional love. To be loved, she had to be the kind of little girl her parents wanted. So the child grew into a woman who imagined she could never be loved for herself.

Remember some of these childhood messages?

- 'Don't be such a cry baby.'
- 'Don't be so childish.'
- 'Don't lose your temper with me. You're behaving like a two-year-old.'
- 'Don't sulk. You're too old to do that.'

Most parents try hard to do their best for their children. But how they cope depends largely on how they were brought up themselves. If they are afraid of showing their more vulnerable feelings, they are likely to want their child to protect herself in the same way. They will want her to keep under control any feelings that might shock, hurt or upset the image they want to have of their child. 'She's such a grown up little girl', her parents say proudly. The message their daughter gets is that there's something wrong in having the spontaneity and openness of a real child.

None of us is ever completely free from our parents' expectations. What matters is whether those expectations can act as an encouragement towards finding our own identity and what we want from life. If we had parents who respected and understood our feelings and were proud of our abilities whatever they happened to be, we were free to grow up to be ourselves. But if we had to grow up hiding the feelings that really mattered to us or felt our parents never 'heard' what they didn't want to hear about us, we need to find ways of understanding those feelings that no one listened to in our childhood.

When Sleeping Beauty is woken by a kiss from her prince, it is a real awakening. When we fall in love, our defences come down and we become vulnerable to those hidden feelings in ourselves. We feel more alive, more interesting and attractive because we are in touch with a more vulnerable and real part of ourselves. And the world around us also seems to come alive because we are seeing it through different eyes.

Every relationship, whether it lasts a week or a lifetime, gives us the chance to continue the process of maturing emotionally. Living happily ever after is the fairy tale's way of saying that we have found the secret of a lasting, loving relationship, which is to love one another for our real selves.

Some questions

There are a series of questions at the end of each chapter to help you discover more of your real self. They will also help you to look at ways in which you may be relating to your partner which are still tied to past relationships.

Give yourself time to answer the questions. Get yourself in a relaxed state and try to ensure there will be no distractions. You and your partner may want to explore the questions together. You may also find it useful to take a few notes to remind yourself afterwards of your answers. If you have a piece of paper and a pencil handy, you may even want to make drawings that represent some of your answers.

Don't think out the answers. Try to let your imagination take over. When you read a question, just let yourself experience any thoughts, feelings or images that come into your mind. Once you have done that, then think about the meaning of those thoughts, feelings or images – and how they relate to you in your present-day life.

You may find yourself coming up with unexpected answers. Don't dismiss them. These answers may be telling you what you need to become aware of so you can understand yourself better and relate to your partner in a better way.

- What type of Sleeping Beauty woman are you?

Think about what is missing in your life, then link it to a part of yourself that is still 'sleeping' which may be preventing you from finding the relationship you want.

- Have you an image of your fairy prince?

Get a picture of what you imagine to be your 'ideal' man. How does this image compare with your teenage fantasies of a dream lover? Are you inwardly still waiting for that imaginary man?

Make a list of the qualities you imagine your ideal man to have. Now compare your real-life partner (or former partners) to him. Do they share some qualities with your 'ideal' man? Do they have other qualities that you value and make up for what they lack in other ways? Or do they always fall short of what you imagine you want in a man?

Ask yourself if what you are searching for in a relationship is realistic or a dream.

- However grown-up we feel, we still retain a childlike part of ourselves. Try and identify that part of yourself. In what situations do you feel the child in you? Do you allow this part of yourself to express itself? Or does the grown-up part of you keep that more spontaneous, open side of your nature under strict control?

Imagine ways your life might benefit if you allowed yourself to be more childlike. Look at the fears you have about that happening and see how they might be overcome.

Make a list of what you imagine being childlike would be like. Then make a second list of what you imagine being childish would be like. Note the differences and think up ways you can enjoy the childlike part of yourself and keep the childish side under control.

- What are your most vivid memories of childhood? Think of three – and then ask yourself what they represent. Can you see aspects of yourself in childhood that are still influencing or restricting your life now?

Try and understand the feelings associated with these memories, what caused them and why they felt so powerful at that time. Now with the grown-up part of yourself, look at these feelings again and see how you could get them more in proportion in your life.

- Do you feel that others don't see or understand the real you? What is that real you like?

Try being alone, so you are cut-off from others' reactions to you. Now think of what you have inwardly that gives you a sense of your own worth. Ask yourself what do you do to 'win' love. Why don't you feel lovable just being yourself? Look at the feelings that make you most anxious or afraid. How do you hide them in yourself?

Why are you afraid of showing others your real self?

- What was expected of you as a child?

Look at which expectations have acted as an encouragement towards getting what you wanted from life. Now look at the expectations that felt like a pressure or a burden. Are you still weighed down by them in your present-day life?

2
Aspects of Love

When we fall in love, it appears to happen out of the blue, when we are least expecting it. But inwardly, it is not so unexpected. Like Sleeping Beauty being awoken from her long sleep by a kiss from her prince, we also have been going through a kind of sleep, a process of internal change that helps us to be ready for the experience. Each relationship also seems like a new beginning, a chance to make a fresh start, because being intimately involved with another person brings about a change in us. It awakens aspects of ourselves that we have lost contact with. As Sleeping Beauty surrounded herself with thorn bushes while she slept, a woman often protects her inner self in a similar way, so no one can get too close to her real feelings. But when she falls in love, those defences come down. Suddenly, she feels intensely alive. She becomes open and vulnerable to feelings and sensations that she'd forgotten existed. It is almost as if she's become another person.

What she has become connected with is a part of herself that goes back to the earliest part of her childhood, when she is likely to have had less need to protect herself. She is re-experiencing a time in her life when she felt safe enough to be herself. When a small child feels secure and loved, she is free to put her whole self into every experience. When she plays, she does so with an intensity and absorption that cuts out all other distractions. She is endlessly curious about herself and the small world around her. Her feelings are as lively, vivid and expressive as she is. She is not inhibited about showing her love towards her parents, just as she is equally open about all her feelings. She can be angry, jealous, possessive, but rather like passing clouds, these moods don't last long. She feels loved for just being herself, so she is able to look at life through her own eyes. She is not weighed down by having to pretend she's someone who fits in or measures up. She doesn't have to deny the feelings that make her feel alive.

That's what the Sleeping Beauty woman re-experiences in herself when she falls in love and is loved in return. A couple in love are playful and endlessly curious about each other. It is as if time stands still when they are together. They have the same absorption in each other that a very young child brings to everything she enjoys. And their feelings are just as spontaneous and intense.

So what goes wrong? How do we lose touch with that part of ourselves that holds so much of our individuality? Why does it usually disappear once the first, euphoric phase in a relationship has worn off?

It happens when expectations start to creep into a relationship, just as they once did between a child and her parents. When a woman begins to see that her partner is not as 'in tune' with her as she first imagined. When she discovers that he has different attitudes and reactions that make her feel he is not the same person as the man she fell in love with. At first, it seemed as if she was all he ever wanted, the centre of his world. But now, when they're together, his attention sometimes wanders, his eyes stray to look at someone else. He can become so absorbed in his work that it is as if she no longer exists. When she tries to tell him how she feels, he looks bewildered, as if he doesn't know what she's making such a fuss about.

This man who had seemed instinctively to 'know' her when they first met, now sometimes behaves like a stranger, who doesn't understand her at all. Sameness is what attracts two people to each other. Having a 'soul mate', someone who seems to share our deepest thoughts and feelings makes us feel understood and connected with someone else. But however much we share with another human being, there are bound to be differences. The awareness that we are different people is what creates a feeling of reality about a relationship that has been missing in that early, euphoric phase. The struggle to understand and overcome differences between ourselves and our partner in a constructive way is what makes a relationship grow up.

Inwardly, each one of us carries an image of a fantasy lover which we project onto our partner when we fall in love. We are attracted to this person because some of his real-life qualities match this internal image, but others we only imagine he possesses. A man also has an image of what his 'dream' woman is like, which to some extent is reflected in the woman he is in love with.

The saying 'Love is blind' is very apt. When we first fall in love, we are so excited by our discovery of this real-life person who has certain qualities which fit our fantasy picture that we are 'blind' to the fact that, in other ways, he is also different from our image of a 'perfect' partner. When differences appear in the relationship, it means that we are beginning to see our partner as a whole person, not someone who is part real and part fantasy.

But the Sleeping Beauty woman finds it hard to let go of her fantasies. Just as she grew up trying to fit an image her parents had of her, she still feels expected to remain the woman her partner fell in love with. She is afraid of him seeing aspects of herself that won't fit that image, just as she was afraid of her parents' rejection if she didn't live up to being the kind of child they wanted. Instead of being able to accept and come to terms with the real-life qualities she discovers in her partner, she also finds it hard to forgive him for not being the man she imagined he was.

Her greatest wish is to be loved for herself, but she is still too afraid that her real self won't be lovable. So once again, she begins to hide her real feelings. Inwardly, she withdraws from her partner to protect herself when she feels hurt or misunderstood. She moves to what feels like a safe emotional distance from him so he cannot reach her most vulnerable feelings. But each time she hides or denies her feelings, she feels cut off from experiencing what it is like to be herself, and her relationship begins to lose the openness and vitality it had when she first fell in love. Inwardly, she feels angry and resentful for again having to live up to a false image and she blames her partner for not understanding how she really feels. But how can he be expected to understand if she reveals so little of her real self? When differences begin to occur between a couple, a relationship has reached the same transition point that Sleeping Beauty had to overcome to leave her childhood behind and take on the challenge of adult life. To overcome this stage, a woman has to be prepared to cope with conflicting feelings about herself and her partner that don't fit in with her romantic fantasies.

In the struggle to get to know each other in a deeper and more realistic way, she is going through a similar conflict that she faced with her parents when she was a teenager. At that time, the struggle was to separate from her dependence on them and to get them to accept her as a person in her own right with her own adult identity. Similarly, she will also reach a point in a relationship where both she and her partner are trying to achieve a balance between their dependence on each other and their need to recognize each other as separate individuals.

A woman needs to risk being different from the person her partner fell in love with if she wants him to know her as she really is. She has to be prepared to risk losing him to win him and to feel his love for her is based on a real knowing of her. At the same time, she has to accept that her lover hasn't lived up to all her expectations. She needs to overcome the disappointment of him letting her down to know how real her love for him is.

Going back to the beginning of life, a time that none of us remember, may not seem to have much relevance to our present-day relationships. Yet psychologists believe the foundations on which we build all future relationships are laid in that first year of a child's life. From the moment of birth, we start to form ways of relating that still have a significant affect on our adult relationships.

A newborn baby still feels part of its mother. It is not aware of having its own identity. It feels totally 'at one' with her. It is a similar sense of 'oneness' that lovers experience in moments when they are so close they feel part of each other. Physically and emotionally they have merged, so it feels as if they have no separate identity.

Before a child learns to walk or talk, it lives in a world of sensations. Its mother's touch is as nourishing as the food she provides. The child feels good enough to touch – and therefore good about itself and being alive. Touch is what gives a baby its first experience outside the womb of being connected with another human being – separate yet not alone.

A mother's smell is also instantly recognizable to a very young child. It is a smell a baby equates with its mother's milk, which gives it a warm feeling and takes away the emptiness inside. Warmth is in a mother's skin as she holds her child in her arms.

A child also needs to be the gleam in its mother's eyes. Seeing itself reflected in her loving gaze is what gives a child its first sense of its own lovableness. It recognizes itself as someone capable of being loved. Satisfying the senses is like satisfying an inner hunger. If a baby feels sufficiently loved from the way its mother responds to her child, it grows up without the need to strive constantly for love. Being loved for ourselves gives us those same feelings. It is the striving to feel lovable that makes us feel empty and dissatisfied.

There remains a yearning in all of us to return to that blissful state, when we felt totally secure and loved. It is like a touchstone that every relationship needs – being able to draw that close to another human being is what reinforces our inner sense of strength and security, however difficult things are in the rest of our lives.

But lovers cannot stay locked in each other's arms for ever, just as a baby cannot remain unaware of having a separate existence from its mother for very long. The awareness that its mother is a separate person comes when a child begins to realize that she doesn't respond automatically to its every need. If it cries, it doesn't get picked up instantly. To a helpless baby, it can feel like its very existence is in danger when it has to wait for its mother to come.

That sense of being separate is highly threatening to a baby whose life is entirely dependent on its mother. It is its first conscious experience of loss. No mother is perfect. There are times when she's not going to respond to her baby in the way it needs. But a good-enough mother is sufficiently in tune with her child to understand and be able to give it enough reassurance that it is loved, even when she is out of sight. It is a process of reassurance that needs to be repeated constantly before the child gains enough inner security to trust in itself when mother is not there. It has acquired enough internal 'nourishment' in terms of good feelings about itself, to feel contented, even when it is on its own.

But if a mother is unable to be responsive and understanding in the way her baby needs, it senses an emotional distance with her. As a young child is unable to communicate in words, it needs to know that its mother is 'in touch' with its feelings so she instinctively knows what her baby needs. But when it senses its mother is more preoccupied with her feelings than its own, it feels cut off from this wordless communication with her. A child who feels emotionally cut off from its mother experiences the fear of being left isolated and alone in a world where it cannot yet take care of itself.

Sometimes a mother cannot provide the absorption in her baby that it needs. Illness or other circumstances in her life may upset this deep emotional bond between them. But a child is too young to understand what has happened to disturb this relationship on which its very survival depends. So it tries to find ways of getting more of its mother's attention and emotional involvement. To do this, a baby becomes more focused on its mother's feelings than its own. Instead of just being itself, it reacts to the way she is. It starts to become a child who tries to 'hang on' to its mother by pleasing her and adjusting to her moods.

A child's deepest fear is losing its mother. So it tries to keep her by becoming the sort of baby she wants, instead of growing up into the child it was meant to be. Every experience of loss connects us with our earliest fears of being separated from our mother or even abandoned by her at the most helpless stage in our lives. Feeling cut off emotionally from someone we depend on brings to the surface hidden anxieties that normally we go to great lengths to protect ourselves from experiencing.

The more vulnerable the Sleeping Beauty woman becomes towards her partner, the greater the fear of losing him is likely to become. She feels so safe and protected in the early, in-love phase of the relationship, when she seemed 'at one' with him. But when she begins to see her lover as a separate person, who has a life apart from her, she becomes afraid of not being able to hold onto him. So she tries to find ways of keeping his attention. She becomes ultra-sensitive to any sign of rejection or emotional withdrawal. She tries to adjust herself to his moods and moulds herself into the kind of woman she imagines he wants, instead of bringing her own individuality into the relationship. She hides her real self because she is afraid of being rejected if her partner knew her as she really is.

No one has a 'perfect' childhood. We all have fears and anxieties that stem right back to our early dependence on our mother and which still profoundly affect our lives. It is the struggle to understand and master these feelings that brings about change in our relationships and a greater maturity in ourselves.

Each relationship gives us the chance to get our fears about rejection and loss more in proportion so they no longer stand in the way of our ability to achieve real intimacy. Just as a small child needs to reach a stage where she does not need constant reassurance to know she is lovable we also need to feel that the same inner security and wellbeing exists within ourselves. In adult terms, this means building up our own individuality so we don't have to seek constant reassurance from our partner that we are loved. It means recognizing and developing our own talents and abilities, getting involved and absorbed in what life has to offer, without depending on our partner to bring us to life. We need to recognize the qualities in ourselves that give us self-confidence and self-worth, instead of relying on someone else's approval or admiration to make us feel good about ourselves.

Having enough of our own 'inner resources' makes it easier to cope with our natural fears of being rejected or losing the person we love. With or without a relationship, we can make the most of every experience life offers us.

Linda, 26, had never been able to sustain a relationship for much longer than a year. The first months with a new lover were always blissful, as she always felt so 'in tune' with her partner. It was almost as if they could read each other's minds.

Then, inexplicably, things between them would start to go wrong. Linda would begin to sense that her lover was not quite so absorbed in her as he had been at first. She would feel anxious and annoyed when he didn't phone exactly when he said he would. Whenever he couldn't see her, she would convince herself that it was because he did not want to be with her. However hard he tried to reassure her, she would feel as if she had lost her trust in him.

Linda's sense of insecurity could be traced back to her first year of life. She had been her parents' first child and until she was nine months old, she was the centre of their lives. But then her mother fell pregnant again. It was a very difficult pregnancy and eventually, she was not well enough to cope with her small daughter. Linda was taken to her mother's sister's house, where she was looked after for several months.

Her parents decided any visits while she was there might unsettle her even further, so Linda did not see them until she was finally brought home to find her mother with a new baby in her arms.

For some time afterwards, Linda became a 'difficult' child. Nothing her parents could do for her made up for the rage and fear she had felt when she had been separated from them. She had been too young to be told that her stay at her aunt's was a temporary one and because her parents didn't visit, she had felt she had been abandoned. Then she had to face what felt like a further rejection when she returned home and found her mother with another child.

Gradually, Linda settled down with her parents again and seemed to have recovered her loving feelings towards them. She became a 'good' child, anxious to please her parents, but inwardly, the wound had not healed. Linda had been left with an intense fear of rejection. In her adult life, when a relationship reached a point where it could have developed into a closer partnership, her childhood fears began to surface again. She began to make demands on her partner that usually caused the relationship to end. She would become clinging and suspicious of what he was up to when he wasn't with her. Any reassurance he tried to give her she found hard to accept.

Linda was still afraid of re-experiencing how she felt as a child when her parents left her. Inwardly, she still feared that she was as unlovable as she had imagined she had become when she'd been 'abandoned' at her aunt's house, only to return home to find she had been 'replaced' by another child.

When she grew up, she found herself wanting to reject any man who tried to get too emotionally close to protect herself from caring too much for someone she secretly feared would leave her.

Linda had been too young to understand why her parents had had to part with her. Unable to put her real feelings into words, she repressed her fears until they surfaced again in her adult relationships. But the difference was that she now had more self-confidence and self-knowledge to help her cope with her fear of rejection. Learning to value herself more and trust that she could survive if her partner left her was the start of a growing-up process. She began to allow herself to experience more emotional closeness in her current relationship because she was less afraid of rejection and loss.

Marie is a 34-year-old woman, who longs to be married and have a family of her own. She came into therapy after a series of failed relationships, all of which ended because none of her partners seemed to want to know her as she really was.

'Everything's fine when a man first falls in love with me,' she said, 'but when that wears off I begin to realize that I've picked someone who hasn't got any emotional strength. I find myself with men who are fine when I'm feeling good about myself. But if I'm feeling low or I get upset or angry, they don't want to know. They back off, leave me alone until I've pulled myself together and become their smiling, fun-loving girlfriend again. I often wonder if any man's capable of loving me for just being me.'

Marie's parents were getting on in years when she was born. They had always had mixed feelings about having a child, but those feelings seemed to vanish when her mother finally became pregnant. Her mother said they were 'over the moon' at her birth. Old family photographs show Marie's parents with expressions of amazement and pride as they stared down at their little daughter. There seemed no doubt about how much they loved her.

What Marie's mother couldn't face were the mixed feelings

that she had always had about having a child. Part of her shied away from the emotional commitment and the fear of having her well-ordered life disrupted by a baby. She felt so guilty about those feelings that she tried to hide them by appearing the 'perfect' mother. Marie also had to appear the 'perfect' baby. Her mother bought her expensive outfits and changed her clothes several times a day. She loved it when people turned round to admire her child when she took her out. What she couldn't stand was her baby's crying. Marie's tears felt like a reproach for her not being the 'perfect' mother she tried so hard to be and this stirred up her sense of guilt. 'If you cried for too long, it really upset me and it disturbed your father', her mother said. 'I used to push you down the end of the garden in your pram, so we couldn't hear you from the house. You always cried yourself to sleep eventually.'

After a few weeks, Marie became a 'good' baby. 'As you got older, I hardly remember you crying at all', her mother told her. 'Everyone said what a model child you were.'

In therapy, a pattern emerged of Marie always hiding her real feelings from her mother so she didn't have to feel 'pushed away' again. Rather than re-experience the anger and despair that she felt at being left alone in her pram to cry, she hid those feelings and became the 'good' daughter her mother could feel proud of.

In her adult life, she picked partners who fell for the cheerful, easy-going impression she gave of herself. But they never appeared to want to know the other, more needy side of Marie's personality. They always seemed to withdraw emotionally from her whenever she got angry or upset. Marie's choice of partners went deeper than repeating a pattern that had begun in the first year of her life. Unconsciously, Marie was trying to master the feelings that had left her inwardly afraid she could not be loved for her real self.

Throughout her life, Marie had felt pushed away by her mother whenever there was any emotional conflict between them. In consequence, she had never felt her mother could love her for herself, but still wanted her to be the nicely dressed, well-behaved little girl she was once so proud of. Marie's anger at what felt like her mother's rejection of her real self surfaced when her boyfriends appeared only to want to know the cheerful, fun-loving part of herself.

Understanding herself better gave Marie a deeper insight

into her choice of partners. She realised that her own fear of not being loved for herself made her pick men who shared her mother's need to push away any feelings that might upset the relationship and spoil the image they had, both of her and of themselves.

Why do we fall in love with men who often turn out to be so similar to ourselves? Why, when we've just met someone, can we get the feeling we've known them all our lives? 'It must be chemistry', we say. Psychology has a different answer.

Like attracts like. You can see this in couples who have a strong physical resemblance to each other and have been attracted to a mirror image of themselves.

At a deeper level, we are also attracted to people who mirror aspects of our personalities, some of which we are aware of. But they are also likely to mirror other qualities that we are more resistant to recognizing in ourselves.

The unconscious part of our minds exerts a great influence over our choice of partners. Each time we meet someone, we communicate at unconscious, as well as conscious, levels. And it is this unconscious 'knowing' of what a person is really like that gives us an intuitive understanding of them that goes deeper than the outer impression that they make. Feeling an instant attraction towards someone we hardly know comes not just from being attracted to their outward appearance, but from an unconscious attraction to similarities in each other's emotional make-up. If the attraction is very powerful, it is likely that we have found someone who also has emotional problems that match our own.

When we first fall in love, we are attracted to qualities in our partner that mirror some of the qualities that we like and appreciate in ourselves. Seeing these aspects of ourselves reflected in someone else connects us with good feelings about ourselves. What is more difficult to accept is that aspects of our partner's personality that we don't like may also be ones that reflect similar, but hidden, aspects of ourselves. They may seem to be the opposite of what we imagine ourselves to be like, because what our partner is mirroring are the qualities we deny most in ourselves.

Psychological health is about change and growth, not feeling trapped by the past or imprisoned by the defences we put up around ourselves. So in psychological terms, we unconsciously choose a partner who can help us become aware of these repressed parts of ourselves that we need to learn to cope with in a more constructive way.

In every relationship, there are bound to be certain things that we don't like about our partner and vice versa. Often we can learn to tolerate, accept and even understand his 'weaknesses' or 'failings'. Through that understanding we can grow to love him in a deeper way. But there will also be some aspects of our partner's character that we cannot forgive. We may blame him for being weak, indecisive, too dependent or for being afraid of emotional commitment. Or we may see his aggressive manner, his moodiness, his self-absorption or his lack of sensitivity as the cause of the problems in our relationship.

If we think about what appears to be our partner's worst 'faults' or 'failings', we may find that they are ones we are the most afraid or ashamed of discovering in ourselves. They may be the same qualities we were brought up to believe were the most unacceptable aspects of our own personalities. They may turn out to be the same 'faults,' 'failings' or 'weaknesses' that we had to repress in childhood in order to fit our parents' image of the child they expected us to be.

For instance, a woman who became afraid of expressing anger in her childhood, may take pride in her ability never to lose her temper. Yet she always seems to get involved with men who fly off the handle at the slightest thing. What makes them even more furious is the cool, detached way in which she behaves when they get into a rage. It is not just her ability to stay emotionally detached during these outbursts that is so infuriating. What her partners are picking up and responding to is her repressed anger that her conscious mind has detached itself from. Instead, she is using her partners to express her hidden anger, as well as their own. What she needs is to recognize her own anger, so she can master her fear of it. Her choice of partners who are in touch with their own angry feelings is an unconscious attempt to allow herself to experience her anger, which, once under her control, can help her to stand up for herself and express her real feelings in a forceful, yet constructive way.

Sandra always found herself being the one who had to 'do everything' in her relationship. When she lived with a man, she was the one who ended up doing more than her fair share of the cooking and housework, even though she went out to work as well. Whenever there was a crisis, she always felt she was the

one who was expected to sort it out and provide her partner
with emotional support. She reached a point where she would
hit the roof if her partner asked her to do even a small thing for
him. She was furious with him for being spoilt and self-
centred. She felt totally 'used' by him.

Sandra was reacting to aspects of her partner that appeared
so extreme to her because they connected up with aspects of
herself that she did not want to recognize.

Sandra had been an only child, who had been told constantly
by her mother that being spoilt and selfish were the worst faults
of all. 'There's nothing worse than a spoilt, only child', she'd
say. 'I'm just thankful you're not like that.' She impressed on
Sandra how fortunate she was as a child and how she must put
others' needs before her own. Her mother had blinded herself
to the fact that Sandra couldn't help being somewhat spoilt and
self-centred. As the only child in the family, she got a lot of
attention and admiration from her parents. But at the same
time, a great deal was expected of her as well.

So Sandra tried to hide her 'worst faults' by becoming a
helpful, self-sacrificing child. She tried to make up for her
shortcomings by becoming the sort of child her parents
wanted, one they could boast about to their friends for being
such an intelligent and likeable little girl.

But Sandra also felt 'used' by them. She felt she had to be a
kind of 'show case' child for her parents to make up for the
shortcomings in their own lives. Sandra had unconsciously
repeated this pattern in her relationship. She was trying to live
up to being the 'perfect' woman, yet she felt totally 'used' by
her partner for expecting her to fulfil this role.

Gradually, she began to realize that her need to 'do everything'
for her partner was to disguise the spoilt, self-centred part of
herself. But this aspect of herself showed itself in ways that she
was not aware of, such as always wanting to be the centre of
attention, her need to be praised and admired for her achievements, and a preoccupation with her own feelings. It made her
demanding in ways she did not like to recognize in herself.

Once Sandra owned these aspects of herself, she began to see
herself differently. She realized that putting herself first did not
automatically make her spoilt or self-centred. In fact, recognizing her own needs lessened her need for attention and
praise. She also began to see that not doing everything for her
partner didn't mean that he would stop loving her.

Sandra had picked a man who had been a spoilt child, accustomed to having things done for him. He saw Sandra's willingness to take over this role in his life as proof that she loved him. But he also had uneasy, sulky feelings about expecting her to do so much. When Sandra began to make demands on him to play a more equal part in the relationship, she found he was prepared to change.

Megan was initially attracted to her lover because he appeared such a strong, self-assured man. He held a position of power in his job and she enjoyed the confident way he handled any crisis at work. It made her feel safe and protected being with such a successful man.

But it didn't take long for Megan to realize that her lover had a different side to him. However well he handled problems at work, he did not seem able to cope with emotional conflicts between them. He backed off any problems in the relationship. Megan could always get the better of an argument and he would often stay late at the office when he knew she was angry with him. It felt to Megan as if her big, strong man was using his job to hide from her.

Megan began to despise her partner for hiding what she saw as emotional weakness under a façade of strength and power. She couldn't seem to stop herself picking fights with him in order to prove what a failure he was in her eyes.

Weakness and failure were what Megan had feared most in her childhood. As a little girl, she had idolized her own father and seen him as a strong, powerful man. But as she got older, she heard her mother talking scornfully about her father as a failure, a weak man who had stayed for years in a safe, underpaid job rather than take any risks in his career. All her parents' arguments seemed to be about their lack of money. Every time, her mother's temper got the better of her father. Gradually, Megan also began to see her father as a man who was unable to stand up for himself.

Megan had repeated the same pattern in her own relationship. She thought she wanted a strong, powerful partner, but in fact what she was also attracted to was her lover's 'weaker' side. Unconsciously, she needed him to appear emotionally weak to protect her from having to experience her fear of her own weaker side. Like her mother, she also turned her anger on her partner and blamed him for the failure of the relationship.

Megan needed to accept her own fear of failure, both in her life and her relationships, before she could begin to relate to her partner in a different and better way. She could then see his 'weaknesses' as a potential strength in their relationship. It was this 'weak' side that contained her partner's real feelings which were hidden behind his outer image of a self-assured, successful businessman.

He needed Megan to accept the more vulnerable man that existed behind the image – his hidden self, whom he wanted her to love.

Some questions

- Remember how it felt when you were in love. Think of those aspects of yourself that surfaced during those times in your life. What is stopping you inwardly from being as spontaneous and lively as you were then?

  Try and get in touch with those feelings in yourself again without having to depend on someone else to make you feel that good about yourself.

- What do you do that is purely for yourself as opposed to fitting in with what others want or living up to someone else's expectations? What do you feel intensely about? What really absorbs your interest in your present day life?

  Start discovering your passion for life by finding interests or activities that would bring you real enjoyment. Then let that enjoyment spread over other areas of your life.

- Think about your attitude to life. Do you wake up thinking about the day's problems and what a struggle it all is? Or are there days when you see your life through different and more hopeful eyes?

  What made the difference inwardly? Think about ways in which you could prevent those hopeful feelings from getting lost.

- How well do you know your partner? Make a list of similarities between you and your partner. Now make a list of the differences between the two of you. Do you understand each better by the similarities or the differences that exist between you? Can you understand and love your partner more by understanding the underlying reasons for his feelings?

Does he know the ways in which you feel differently from him? If not, why not? How do you hide these differences? And how does that make you feel?

Try talking to your partner, not about your differences, but why it is so difficult to talk about these differences that exist between the two of you. You need to work at bringing down the emotional barrier that prevents you from really telling each other how you feel.

• What good qualities in your partner's personality reflect aspects of yourself?

What qualities of his that really irritate or anger you connect with aspects of yourself you would prefer not to recognize? Instead of blaming yourself, can you 'own' these more difficult parts of yourself?

• Can you recognize a pattern of relating in your relationships? Do you come up against the same emotional barrier or continue to make the same mistakes in each relationship?

Compare the way you relate to your partner to the way you related to your parents or siblings in your childhood. Can you find similarities? Are you continuing to repeat a pattern of relating that won't stop until you understand why it is happening?

3
The Myth of Sex

Sex can seem like a real awakening in a woman's life. She can feel completely taken over by her sexual feelings when she falls in love. What convinces her that she has met the right man is the strength of the sexual attraction that exists between them which overwhelms all other feelings. But once the idyllic, honeymoon stage in the relationship is over, she begins to see that she has been caught up in a fantasy. Sex has not brought her the closeness and intimacy that she is looking for. She may even begin to wonder what she ever saw in the man she had thought was so right for her. She had fallen for the modern day myth that sex would transform her life.

We put so much importance on sexuality that it is no wonder sex rarely lives up to our expectations. Like Sleeping Beauty whose looks remained unchanged while she sleeps, a woman may feel that she needs to stay youthful and beautiful in order to be sexually attractive. It is natural for a woman to want to make the best of her appearance, but the Sleeping Beauty woman is likely to have a far greater preoccupation with her looks.

Instead of having the inner confidence to feel her sexual attractiveness is an intrinsic and natural part of herself, she still regards it as something that she can acquire by going on a diet or buying different make-up. Just as when she was a teenager, she is still trying to turn herself into an idealized image of a sexually attractive woman. No matter how much sexual experience she has had, her attitude towards sex has not fundamentally changed since her adolescence. She is still likely to be looking for the same sexual excitement in a relationship that she experienced the first time she fell in love.

When she falls in love, the power of her sexual instincts overwhelms and dominates the rest of her feelings. Inwardly, a part of her is still looking for the kind of relationship that she believed would bring her true love when she was a teenager. What she finds difficult is transforming the sexual attraction she feels for her partner into a more lasting and mature sexual relationship.

The Sleeping Beauty fairy tale warns of the dangers of a young girl getting involved in sexual relationships before she has gained enough emotional maturity to understand her sexuality. It shows how the sleeping princess is surrounded by thorn bushes to prevent suitors reaching her before she is ready for an adult relationship. With her head full of romantic fantasies, a teenager can easily fall for the modern-day myth that sex will 'magically' transform her life. She imagines that having a sexual relationship will turn her into a grown-up, so she can leave those awkward adolescent years behind and become a self-confident and desirable woman. She may begin to have sexual relationships before she is grown up enough to understand and cope with her sexual feelings, so they seem overwhelming and out of proportion to the rest of her emotional development. She is using sex to try and make up for an emotional maturity she does not yet possess.

A young girl's sexual feelings are what drive her towards making the difficult transition from childhood into adult life. They help transform her from being the child she once was into a woman. But finding her own, grown-up identity, which includes her sexuality, is a gradual process, not one that happens the instant she falls in love.

A teenager may feel that what she wants most is to wave goodbye to her parents and her home, set up in her own place and start to lead a grown-up life. Any sign that her parents are still treating her like a child is met with anger and scorn. Yet, inwardly, a young girl is not nearly as confident about separating from her family as she makes out. What really angers her is that there is still a part of her that wants to cling to her childhood dependency on her parents, though usually she blames others for trying to prevent her from growing up. She has reached a point in her life where her inner self feels pulled in two directions – she wants to become independent and have a different life from her parents, yet there is still a need in her to remain the same person as she has always been in order to feel safe and protected. Just as Sleeping Beauty had to explore unknown parts of the castle to discover the spinning wheel that represented her reaching sexual maturity, so a teenager has to make a similar journey into the 'unknown' adult world to discover her grown-up self.

But for all that she is likely to gain by making that transition, she still has to overcome the profound loss of her childhood and her role in her family as her parents' little girl. Instead of allowing herself time to come to terms with these feelings and gradually learning to stand on her own feet, a teenager may plunge into sexual relationships as a way of transferring her childhood dependency on her parents onto her lover. She blots out the pain involved in making a real separation from her family, which would help her to cope with her fears about separation and loss in her adult relationships.

The Sleeping Beauty woman may continue to use sexual relationships as an escape from deeper anxieties about herself. The excitement of sex makes her 'forget' her inner lack of self-confidence and self-worth. She is still caught up in a fantasy about romantic, sexualized love, which as a teenager, she imagined would transform her life.

If she expects too much from the sexual attraction that exists between herself and her partner at the start of the relationship, their passion for each other is unlikely to last. Sex has been used to escape the more complicated task of gaining real emotional maturity, which comes from sorting out her confused feelings about herself. Otherwise the real awakening comes when she discovers that she has nothing in common with her partner apart from sexual desire.

Sexual attractiveness is an indefinable quality that doesn't depend on external appearances. It is part of a woman's individuality. Her attractiveness is in her voice, her gestures, the way she moves her body. It is in her being able to be her real self.

This kind of woman has an openness and an enthusiasm towards life, which attracts people to her. She does not have to protect herself by appearing so independent and self-sufficient that she seems not to need anyone. She can show her vulnerability to those she trusts and cares about. She does not depend on someone else to tell her she is attractive before she feels good about herself. How inwardly confident she is about her sexuality depends a great deal on her parents' attitude towards sex when she was growing up.

In adolescence, a young girl needs to feel that her sexual feelings are accepted by her parents as a normal part of her development. Then she can accept and appreciate her sexuality in the same way as she values other aspects of herself. But a teenager can feel that her parents don't welcome or appreciate her emerging sexuality. They may ignore any signs of her physical maturity. She may also have grown up in a family where even mentioning the word sex caused an awkward atmosphere in the house. The message she gets is that sex will only get her into trouble and cause a rift between herself and her parents, who want her to remain their own little girl. Sex no longer seems an enjoyable part of her parents' marriage and she desperately wants to fall in love to prove that it won't be like that for her. What she is looking for is a partner who will give her the confidence that she has not yet found in herself.

A young girl looks first and foremost to her mother to provide her with a role model for her own womanhood. If she has a mother who values her own sexuality, her daughter is likely to grow up with the ability to appreciate the sexual part of her own nature. She won't be so overwhelmed by her sexual feelings that she is driven to get involved in unsatisfactory or even disastrous relationships and behave in irrational ways. But a teenager, whose mother repressed her own sexuality or who has never really grown up in her attitude towards sex, is confused about her own sexual feelings. She is caught between trying to repress what feels like a threatening and unacceptable part of herself, while wanting to experience the excitement of a real-life sexual relationship.

A teenager lives in a world of fantasies about sexual love based on the glamourized relationships she sees in films and reads about in romantic fiction. She tries to turn herself into a sexually desirable woman by dressing like her favourite film or pop star. She may invent a sexual image for herself to escape the dreary and off-putting image her mother has given her of womanhood. She has fallen for the modern-day myth that sex will transform her life.

Peggy, 19, loved her mother, but she was also angry with her. She was a good-looking woman, but she hid her attractiveness by not bothering with her appearance and she even made fun of her own looks. She seemed to want to discourage any sexual interest, particularly from her husband.

From what Peggy observed and overheard about her parents' marriage, her mother seemed to be bored and turned-off by sex. Her mother's attitude towards sex had its affect on her teenage daughter, who desperately wanted to feel sexually attractive and confident because inwardly she felt just the reverse.

Peggy blossomed when boys started to notice her. She spent a great deal of time on her appearance and she loved to flirt. Getting male attention and making them desire her was the way she proved to herself that she was sexually attractive. She saw her boyfriends as objects who could make her feel good about herself. She fell in love easily and she imagined every relationship would turn out to be a great romance. She equated sexual desire with love.

Peggy was living out her teenage fantasies about sex. She could forget her adolescent insecurities when she felt attractive and desirable to a boyfriend. She absorbed her boyfriends' personalities. Their opinions became hers. She found herself liking and disliking the same things as they did. She felt worthless and unattractive whenever a relationship broke up.

Peggy was using sexual relationships to avoid facing her anxieties about growing up. But without having discovered any real sense of her own adult self, she became dependent on her boyfriends to give her an identity.

What Peggy needed was more space in her life for self-discovery, so she could start letting go of her teenage fantasies and her fear of growing up into a woman like her mother. Instead of being obsessed with her relationships, she needed to develop other areas of her life. By discovering what she wanted from her life, she would begin to build up a separate identity and get a more confident and realistic sense of her own self. The danger is that she will continue to go from one relationship to the next to keep trying to prove to herself that by being sexually desirable she is also capable of being loved.

Every woman has a fantasy about being awakened by her 'prince', the lover she has been waiting for to transform her life. It exists in the part of herself that has stayed 'asleep' since her adolescence, when she dreamed of the 'perfect' partner who would rescue her from the hard struggle of growing up.

So who is this dream lover? Who does this imaginary partner represent?

He is likely to be her father, the first hero figure in a little girl's life, who, in her child's eyes, would love her for ever and never let her down. Even when she becomes a woman, a part of her still hangs on to the fantasy that somewhere a man exists who can make her feel just as safe and secure.

Every sexual partner initially carries some of a woman's fantasies about her dream lover. But as she gets to know her real-life partner, she begins to sort out and relate to his real qualities rather than the ones she imagined he possessed. She starts to love him for the person he is.

But if a woman is still inwardly 'in love' with her dream lover, she will find it harder to accept the disappointment when she discovers that her real-life partner is different from the image she had had about him. She may be so disillusioned that she falls out of love with her current lover and into love with another man who appears to fit her fantasy of an ideal partner. But by clinging to her illusions, she always withholds a part of herself from her real-life relationships so none has a proper chance to develop into a deeper partnership.

It is not just the woman herself who has been unable sufficiently to let go of her childhood illusions in order to experience real and more fulfilling adult relationships. She may be still trapped by her father's reluctance to let his little girl grow up into a woman. Sleeping Beauty's father went to great lengths to prevent his daughter from pricking her finger on the spinning wheel, which in the fairy tale symbolizes her reaching physical maturity. And in doing so, he was behaving like many fathers who want to keep their daughter's love and admiration for themselves. Remaining a daddy's girl is a temptation a woman faces, especially when her father did not want to lose her to another man.

A father is the first, male role model in his daughter's life and her relationship with him plays an important part in her development as a woman and the way she relates to men when she grows up. Even a small child recognizes her father as a person who gives her qualities that are different from the ones her mother provides. His touch, smell, the feel of his body, the sound of his voice and the boisterous way he plays with her convey an 'otherness' that fascinates her. By recognizing his male qualities, she begins to define her own femininity, which she discovers in contrasting the differences between them. Her father's appreciation of her helps her to enjoy her emerging femininity and gives her confidence in her ability to be loved by a man.

Even if a woman's father was absent during her childhood or was someone she never knew, she would still have created a childhood image of an ideal father, whom she imagined would give her the love and acceptance she longed for. When she grows up, this fantasy figure becomes the 'perfect' lover she is always searching for.

Being 'in love' with daddy is a natural phase in childhood, and equally a father enjoys being the most important man in his small daughter's life. As he is usually a more distant figure to a child than her mother, he can also appear more interesting and exciting to a little girl. Even if he's a strict father or appears emotionally withdrawn, she never really gives up trying to please him and win his love. Waiting for father to come home from work becomes an occasion that she longs for. She anticipates the expression of pleasure on his face when he sees her as he walks in the door. She may regard her father as more fun or more understanding than her mother, who is likely to be more involved in the tougher, more practical aspects of bringing a child up. Mother won't stand any nonsense, but she can twist daddy round her little finger.

So a little girl comes to regard her relationship with father as livelier and more enjoyable than the one she has with her mother. She grows up imagining that only men bring out the best in her.

A daughter also needs to identify with her father to recognize her own, masculine qualities, which will help her separate from the safe, contained world of her childhood and take on the challenge of an independent, adult life. But she needs to get her father's influence over her in proportion. The illusion about him as a hero figure has to be shattered before she can see him as a real person with weaknesses as well as strengths. Then she can love him for his real qualities and appreciate what he does have to offer her, which will help her to let go of her romantic fantasies and relate in a real way to partners in her adult life.

It is during a teenager's transition from childhood into adult life that a young girl usually begins to wake up to realize that her father is not the 'perfect' man she imagined and becomes angry because her hero has let her down. From imagining him to be a strong, protective man, he now appears to be just the reverse. Because she's afraid of losing her father's affection and her place in his life, she may protect both him and herself from facing her conflicting feelings about him. A part of her still wants to cling to her early childhood image of him and remain daddy's girl, so her anger towards him for 'failing her' gets taken into her adult relationships. She divides men into two types, the ones she admires and even idolizes and the others who let her down. In her relationships, she is likely to start off expecting too much from her partner, so, like father, he is bound to fail her.

A teenage girl also gains confidence in her emerging sexuality from her father. If he accepts it in a natural and encouraging way, she will feel confident enough to look for a partner of her own. She is also more able to work out a different and more grown-up relationship with her father, which is based on loving his real qualities. She has turned her childhood hero into a real-life and fallible human being.

But a father often can't cope with his own complicated feelings towards his teenage daughter. He becomes alarmed when he sees that she is growing up fast and that it won't be long before he will lose his 'little girl'. Rather than face his own feelings about this loss, he begins to distance himself both physically and emotionally from his daughter. He pushes her away whenever she tries to get close to him. 'You're too big for good night kisses and cuddles now', he tells her.

To a young girl, this can seem like a rejection of her emerging, grown-up self. It happens at a time when she is likely to feel gauche, awkward and intensely vulnerable about herself; she needs her father's reassurance to begin to feel confident about herself. She is too immature to understand her father's struggle with his own feelings. Instead she feels devastated that the most important male figure in her life no longer seems to appreciate or understand her. Because it seems as if her sexual development has caused this rift between them, she feels even more unsure about her grown-up self. To try and prove she can still be loved, she rushes into her first sexual relationship.

Jenny, 28, recalls her bewilderment when her father stopped cuddling her when she reached puberty. The dad who had enjoyed romping and play-fighting with her when she was small, suddenly turned into a stern-faced father, who always seemed to hide behind his newspaper whenever she tried to climb onto his lap.

What made this change in him harder to bear was that Jenny's mother had always found it hard to show physical affection towards Jenny and her younger sister. So she had turned to her father to give her the physical reassurance that she was a lovable little girl.

Jenny says: 'I can't remember my mother touching me much when I was a child. She was always doing something in the house, as if her busy-ness would keep the physical barrier between us. So my father's cuddles became supremely important to me. The way dad looked at me was special too. I could actually see his love and pride in me reflected in his eyes.'

Jenny could not understand what she had done to make her father suddenly push her away. What made it worse was that her sister, who is six years younger, was still getting the hugs and kisses from their dad. Jenny began to feel that her sexuality had caused the rift between them. Her father seemed to resent this sign that his little girl was growing into a woman and Jenny felt hurt and angry with him for not understanding how much she needed his encouragement and approval.

Jenny started to get sexually involved with boys when she was sixteen. Petting excited her because of the physical contact that she had felt deprived of in childhood. It was also a way of getting her own back on her father, who was furious whenever she stayed out late with a boyfriend. She wanted to hurt him for letting her down.

Jenny says: 'A girlfriend and I used to go with our boyfriends down a lover's lane my father had forbidden me to visit. And one night, dad found me down there, kissing a boy in the shadows. Dad shone a torch in our faces, then hauled me off home. It was a terrifying experience because he was so angry. I felt ashamed, but excited at the same time. I felt my father must still care about me if I could make him so angry.'

When Jenny grew up, she outwardly appeared to have made the transition into adult life. She had a good career in the fashion industry and she was a friendly, popular young woman with a busy social life. But in her sexual relationships, she was still searching for the father she had been so close to when she was a little girl. Every man she became involved with always seemed to let her down.

Jenny had grown up feeling so uncertain about her sexuality that she could never 'let go' of herself in love-making. She enjoyed the physical intimacy of sex because it gave her the holding and touching that her childhood relationship with her mother had lacked. But she was too afraid of experiencing rejection again if she allowed herself to be emotionally vulnerable to the men in her life.

Inwardly Jenny was still struggling to grow up emotionally. She needed to let go of her childhood, idealized image of her father, so she could forgive him for failing her. She could then see his apparent reaction to her grown-up self, not as a rejection, but as his vulnerability towards a sexually-maturing daughter, especially when he had a wife who was physically cold.

By understanding both her parents better, Jenny also gained more insight into herself. She began to have a different and more rewarding relationship with her current partner by becoming more emotionally open, instead of constantly protecting herself from the rejection she had always imagined was bound to come. She was able to allow more real and lasting feelings to develop between them by seeing her partner as a person with his own individual qualities, not simply as a carbon copy of the father who had seemed to let her down.

Giving up illusions isn't easy. Having an image of a perfect relationship goes back to a time when we imagined we had perfect parents and life could always be as idyllic as it seemed at certain moments in childhood. Maybe those were only fleeting moments, but we clung onto them in memory, always wanting to recreate them in our adult relationships because they made us feel safe and loved. But staying 'asleep' in the past means we can miss the possibilities that present-day relationships offer. We never put our whole selves into any experience, as a part of us is still waiting for our childhood dream of meeting the 'perfect' partner to come true. Fantasies are an important part of our internal world. Just as Sleeping Beauty needed to fall asleep to prepare herself for adult life, we also need the same kind of inner reverie to sort out past experiences and move on to the next phase in our lives.

Daydreaming can be about reliving these experiences in our inner world in an imaginative way. It is a way that we search for meaning in what happens in our lives. In our fantasies also we can become the kind of person we would like to be. We can dream that we have the 'perfect' partner and the 'perfect' relationship. But fantasies can also become a substitute for reality. They become an escape from the difficulties that are an inevitable part of all relationships and a way of avoiding facing reality about ourselves. Like Sleeping Beauty, we can stay forever young, beautiful and problem-free in our fantasies. But if we live too much in a fantasy world, we also risk becoming real-life Sleeping Beauties, sleeping our lives away.

Letting go of fantasies is a struggle if a woman has never felt confident about her grown-up self. If she grew up feeling awkward or ashamed about her sexual feelings or lacking confidence in her adult identity, she is tempted to stay asleep in fantasies in which she can become the kind of woman she secretly would like to be. In her daydreams, she remains safe and secure with her dream lover, who will never tire of her sexually or stop loving her. Her fantasies are her protection against facing up to her uncertainties about her ability to be loved for her real self.

This kind of woman may have grown up in a family where

sexuality was repressed. So instead of allowing her sexual feelings to grow up in a natural way along with the rest of her emotional development, that part of herself had to remain hidden and secret. The one place it felt safe to have sexual feelings was in her fantasies.

When she falls in love for the first time, it feels as if her fantasies are about to become reality. She is swept away by the excitement of experiencing these 'forbidden' feelings that have been 'sleeping' inside her for so long and seem so overwhelming once they emerge in a real-life relationship. But because her sexual feelings were so repressed while she was growing up, they have remained split off and less mature than the rest of her emotions. What she tries to do is live out her fantasies, which means that her relationships are likely to end in disappointment. No partner can live up to being the lover whom she has created in her imagination.

When a woman stops trying to live out her sexual fantasies, she becomes more tolerant and accepting of what a relationship does have to offer her. She lets go of her romanticized expectations and begins to accept herself and her partner for their real qualities. She becomes more open and spontaneous in love-making, as she is less afraid of showing that she is not the sexually confident woman she can only pretend to be in fantasy. She can allow herself to appear awkward, embarrassed and sometimes insecure. She can tolerate love-making not being the 'perfect' experience she imagined. She can even allow for it to go wrong at times without feeling that she is with the wrong partner. She begins to discover how to experience and enjoy her real sexuality.

Gemma, 26, often thought sex was a word that didn't exist in her parents' vocabulary. It was such an unmentionable subject that, as a child, she felt an acute sense of embarrassment just watching a love scene on television when her parents were in the same room.

As an adolescent, she tried to disguise the physical signs of her own sexuality. She didn't wear a bra until she was fifteen and stayed in childish socks and flat shoes when her friends were into wearing tights and high heels.

According to Gemma's parents, she changed almost over-night at the age of sixteen, when she started dating a boy they didn't approve of. The socks went straight in the waste-paper basket to be replaced by sheer black tights and heels. Her

parents were convinced that their 'nicely brought up' daughter
had turned into a slut.

They blamed her boyfriend for the change in her. In their
eyes, he was a troublemaker, who was 'only after one thing'.
He would ruin her life, her parents warned, although still the
word 'sex' was not mentioned.

Gemma's boyfriend wasn't as bad as her parents' painted
him. He was trying to 'make it' as a pop singer and Gemma
thought he was almost too wonderful to be true when she
watched him on stage at local gigs. She could see how other
girls envied her for having this exciting, sexy-looking lover. He
was her 'prince' who seemed to have stepped right out of her
secret, childhood fantasies.

Gemma was living out her fantasies as a reaction against her
parents attitude towards sex. Choosing a sexual partner they
didn't approve of was a way of expressing her anger towards
them for not accepting the sexual part of her nature. Being with
such a local heartthrob made Gemma feel attractive and
lovable. But she lost all confidence in herself when her
boyfriend left her for another girl.

Gemma's sexual relationships followed a similar pattern.
She always found herself attracted to men who were exciting
but irresponsible, which meant her parents never approved of
them. That way, she continued to keep her sexuality separate
from her family life. Just as sex had been an unmentionable
subject when she was a child, she never discussed her sexual
relationships with her parents.

Gemma also kept her sexual feelings as a separate part of
herself, cut off from the rest of her personality. This meant that
she divided her relationships between two types of men – those
she found sexually exciting, but with whom she had little else
in common and usually ended up letting her down, and more
reliable, responsible types, whom she liked as friends, but not
lovers.

What Gemma needed to realize was that being different
from the image her parents wanted her to live up to did not
make her unlovable, just as having sexual feelings did not turn
her into a 'bad' or 'irresponsible' young woman. By developing a different and more accepting attitude towards her
sexuality, she would be able to experience her sexual feelings as
a natural and enjoyable part of her relationships which she
no longer needed to be secretly ashamed of.

Remember how babyish we become when we first fall in love –
the baby talk, those pet names we chose for each other, the cute,
little childlike gifts we can't resist buying for our partner? When
we fall in love we become childlike. We re-experience those
spontaneous, lively feelings we had in early childhood when we
felt 'special' to our parents and also idolized them. What we
wanted most was to be like them. Just as we have to experience
disillusionment about our parents as part of our growing-up
process, we can experience the same disillusionment when we
begin to see our lover as a different person from the man we fell in
love with.

When this transition point between fantasy and reality is
reached, a relationship begins to grow up. We may discover
whether we actually can love this man who has fallen from his
pedestal. This doesn't mean that we have to leave behind the
childlike fun and playfulness in a relationship. But, at the same
time, a couple also need to turn the early sexual excitement they
experienced together into real emotional intimacy if sex is to
continue to be a lively and passionate part of their relationship.

A woman can experience her most intense feelings in love-
making. Being 'penetrated' or 'entered' by a man is not just a
description of a physical act. She reveals her naked self, both
physically and emotionally to her lover. She allows not only her
body, but the layers of protection that she has built up around her
deepest feelings to be 'penetrated' when they make love. She
allows him to 'enter' her real self.

By 'opening' herself to her lover, a woman is also open to
change in herself. By allowing him to know her as she really is, she
is also allowing him to reach her deepest, most vulnerable
feelings. It is not easy for a woman to allow herself such emotional
openness, however secure or loving a relationship appears. She
needs to trust her partner before she can risk exposing feelings
that matter most to her without fearing that she might be hurt or
rejected by him.

Sleeping Beauty's prince was prepared to struggle through the
thorn bushes that surrounded her castle to reach the sleeping
princess. A woman also needs her lover to be prepared to struggle
through the layers of protection she has built around her most
vulnerable feelings to know her as she is. In a real-life relationship, this represents the struggle to develop real understanding
between herself and her partner in which she needs to play an
equal part. She does that by facing up to her fears that surface

when she becomes emotionally close to someone she cares about. For the closer she allows her partner to get to her, the more she has to cope with her fear of not being loved for herself.

Understanding why we protect ourselves from being known for our real selves reduces the need to protect ourselves so much. It is like gradually unwrapping layers of protective clothing that we have worn to try and protect ourselves from getting too deeply hurt. But those layers of protection have also cut us off from feelings that help us relate to our own partner in a more fulfilling way.

What always seemed to ruin Jill's relationships was sex. Her affairs usually began with a great deal of passion. For the first few months, all she seemed to think about was making love with her partner and she was never satisfied until he showed the same obsessive desire for her. She tried so hard to be the perfect sexual partner, so her lover couldn't resist her.

But hidden behind Jill's sexuality was a great deal of unexpressed anger that went back to her early teens when her father had left her mother for another woman. At the time, her family had marvelled at how well Jill had appeared to cope with her parents' marriage break-up. She had put on such a brave face and helped her mother to cope with hardly any show of emotion. What she had hidden, even from herself, was her anger and grief at her father's loss and her desire to punish him for abandoning her.

These feelings surfaced in her sexual relationships. As each of her affairs progressed, she would find herself resenting having to try so hard to please her partner. Sex was what kept him interested in her. When they made love, it was his satisfaction and pleasure, not hers, that mattered. She began to long to feel loved for herself.

Instead of seeing how much she was responsible for creating this role in her relationship, Jill blamed her partner for his selfishness and lack of feeling. Her anger would surface and there would be constant rows in which she would accuse her lover of not caring enough for her and not understanding her real feelings. What she was reliving was her rage against her father for leaving the daughter he had claimed to care so much about.

Jill was unconsciously setting up relationships in which she could re-experience this childhood anger, which was preventing her from having closer relationships. Without realizing it, she always made sure her relationships broke up before there was any deep involvement, so she didn't have to face the same hurt as when her father had left.

Understanding the underlying reason for her anger helped Jill to begin to break this pattern in her relationships. She needed to experience and come to terms with the feelings she had repressed when her father left before she felt free to risk a deeper involvement with another man.

Words used to describe the sexual act, such as 'penetration' and 'fertilization', also describe other forms of 'intercourse' between a couple. A woman can feel penetrated by something her lover says to her that gets right through to her deepest feelings. What he says may resound inside her like a shock because he has glimpsed an aspect of her that she normally tries to hide from others or protect herself from recognizing. He has got through to her most vulnerable feelings and made her feel naked and defenceless.

When a woman becomes emotionally 'open' to her partner, she takes the risk of him getting through to feelings she may not like facing in herself. The temptation is to withdraw emotionally to protect her real self from feeling so exposed. But if she can remain emotionally open, she can begin to see that her partner's understanding of her has given her a different and deeper awareness of herself. It is as if a fertilization has taken place – an aspect of herself that she has repressed, has been brought to life, which brings about change in her. What comes into the open are feelings that she may be ashamed of or qualities in herself she is afraid will show her to be different from the image of herself she wants her partner to have. But if she realizes that he can accept and even understand these aspects of herself that she wants to reject, she can begin to have a different attitude towards herself. She may find that she becomes more lovable to her partner when she allows him to see more of her real self. She becomes less afraid of being emotionally open because she feels her lover cares enough about her as a person to want to know her as she really is.

Some questions

- What is your image of a sexually attractive woman? Is it similar to the one you had when you were a teenager?

  Can you imagine yourself being sexually attractive as an

older woman? What characteristics do you have that don't depend on your physical appearance that would continue to make you feel an attractive person, whatever age you happen to be?

Look at the qualities you possess as an individual that can make you an attractive and desirable woman.

- Think about your first sexual relationship. How much was it linked with your need to separate from your parents and feel grown up?

  How much have you been using relationships ever since to avoid facing your fears about being independent and standing on your own feet?

- How did your parents treat sex when you were growing up? Do you imagine they had a fulfilling sex life? How did they react to your emerging sexuality when you were in your teens?

  Ask yourself how much of their attitude still affects your own ability to enjoy a sexual relationship. Do you still inwardly think there is something 'bad' or 'wrong' about having sexual feelings?

- How much of a daddy's girl are you still? Is there a part of you that is still searching for a man who can live up to the hero figure that your father once appeared to you? Look at the ways your partner is similar to your father. Then look at the ways in which he is different. If the similarities outweigh the differences, it is likely your childhood attachment to your father is still strong.

  Do you tend to put men on a pedestal – and then feel that they let you down? If that happens, look at ways your father let you down in the past. Were you able to confront him with your real feelings, or are you still punishing other men in your life for your father's failures? You need to come to terms with the reality of your relationship with your father to free yourself from an endless search for your fairy prince.

- Are your expectations about sex too high – or too low? Do you find it difficult to keep the passion alive in every relationship you have?

  Look at what defences you put up in love-making. Do you fake orgasms or pretend to be enjoying yourself more than you are? Think about what stops you being open with your partner by showing your real feelings to him in love-making.

- Do you allow yourself to be open with your partner in other ways? What stops you letting him get through to you emotionally?

  Think of the times when you felt vulnerable as a child. Were you made to feel awkward or even ashamed of those feelings? Is that same fear stopping you from risking real emotional closeness with your partner?

  What makes you feel vulnerable towards him now? Think about how you could safely talk to him about this. Helping him to understand how you feel can be the start of a process of really getting to know each other.

4
Promiscuity or Passion?

Sophie, 28, had an aunt, who for as long as she could remember had a succession of corgi dogs. When one died, within forty-eight hours, she always replaced it with another almost identical dog. Apart from the first corgi her aunt had, Sophie could not remember anything that distinguished one dog from the next.

In a way, they were all the same dog – not animals with their own particular characters, but replacements for her aunt's first, much-loved dog. Each one even grew as snappy and spoilt as her original pet. 'I just can't bear the pain of losing a dog', her aunt once told her. 'I don't know how I'd survive it if I didn't get another dog to take its place.'

When Sophie looks back on her own life, she sees that she has acted in a similar way in her relationships. Whenever a relationship ended, she was distraught for a short while. Then she would 'pull herself together' and find another partner. She even took pride in her ability not to be really hurt by any man. Looking back, she even got confused over some of her former boyfriends' names. Like her aunt's succession of dogs, each new lover was a replacement for the last.

Sophie never allowed enough space between her relationships to know how she really felt about the one that had just ended. She was going into one relationship after the other to protect her from experiencing any feelings of loss. This relationship pattern began after her father's sudden death when Sophie was seventeen. The shock of losing him was so great that for a long time she felt completely numb. Her mother had been so devastated that Sophie had repressed her own grief to look after her. She was in the midst of struggling with all her teenage uncertainties and conflicts about growing up, and the loss of her father at the same time was too much for her to cope with.

When she fell in love for the first time a year later, the intensity of her sexual feelings seemed to bring her to life again. But Sophie was more in love with the excitement of her first romance than her boyfriend. She was living out a fantasy about what she imagined love to be, while inwardly she was protecting herself against developing any deeper feelings towards her boyfriend which would have stirred up her fears about losing him.

When he left to go to university, she cut off her feelings for him in the same way she had distanced herself from the loss of her father. She felt nothing when he stopped writing because she had already fallen in love again.

Sophie's relationships followed a similar pattern. At the start of each affair, she always fell passionately in love. But she always found herself involved with men who, for one reason or another, were not in a position for a long-term relationship. In that way, she protected herself against real emotional involvement.

Sophie had substituted promiscuity for real sexual passion. She seduced men for the satisfaction it gave her when they found her attractive. But she always found herself falling out of love when her romantic fantasies about her lovers began to wear thin. She prided herself on her independence, her ability not to hang on to a man when their relationship started to 'go wrong'. Inwardly, she was afraid of becoming emotionally dependent on her partner in the same way as she had depended on her father's love. Even though it was eleven years since her father's death, Sophie still had not mourned him. She needed to become more aware of the feelings which she had repressed since he died, instead of going from one relationship to the next to avoid facing them.

When Sleeping Beauty reaches the transition between childhood and adult life she falls asleep and is only woken by her prince when she is ready for a grown-up relationship. Her sleep represents the inward process of change that she is going through in order to mature into a woman.

At the end of each phase in life, we go through a similar process of change. The turbulent emotions, the mood swings and the long periods of dreamy introspection that a teenager experiences are the outward signs of the inner changes that are taking place in a young girl on the threshold of becoming an adult. A woman can go through similar emotions when she reaches the mid-life crisis, which is sometimes referred to as the 'change of life'.

Coming to terms with old age is a transition in which a woman has to start preparing for the end of her life. She needs time to look back over the phases in her life, so she can integrate her experiences and find meaning in them.

Each phase represents both loss and gain: loss of childhood for the teenager about to become a woman; loss of youth for the woman about to become middle-aged; loss of career and the gradual loss of physical strength as we reach retirement age. What we can gain at each phase is maturity, if we allow ourselves time to integrate past experience and come to terms with the changes we are going through. Change is both challenging and threatening because it involves loss, which stirs up our deepest anxieties and fears. But if we're prepared to understand and master those feelings, we gain a deeper sense of ourselves. In the struggle of coming to terms with changes in our lives, we experience what it is like to be our real selves.

Translated into real-life experience, Sleeping Beauty's sleep represents the time we need to sort out the inner conflicts that change creates. By understanding and coming to terms with past experiences, we integrate that understanding, so it becomes a part of ourselves. Once we have learnt from our experiences we can let go of them inwardly and move on to the next phase in our lives. Like Sleeping Beauty, we allow ourselves time to go through a process of change before we are ready to be awakened to experience life in a different and more fulfilling way than we have before.

When Sleeping Beauty woke up to find her prince, she had gained enough maturity to separate from her childhood relationship with her parents and begin a grown-up relationship with her prince.

Each time a relationship ends, a woman also needs to allow herself time to sort out her feelings. She needs to integrate the experience, make it a part of herself, so she can move on to her next relationship with a greater awareness of herself and the kind of man she needs. When a relationship goes wrong, it is natural to want support and a shoulder to cry on. But finding a new lover can be a way of trying to escape from the feelings of failure her last relationship has left her with. Those feelings don't get left behind when she starts her next relationship. Instead they become part of an underlying anxiety and insecurity she feels about herself. She wants her new lover to help her forget the past and make her feel safe and confident about herself again. But however much reassurance he tries to give her, her inner doubts remain. The only way she can gain real emotional security is by allowing herself to experience the feelings she had been running away from. By understanding and being able to master her own fears and anxieties, she becomes less in need of using a relationship as an emotional prop.

The failure of a relationship may strip a woman of her self-confidence and self-worth. But instead of depending on someone else to restore her confidence, she can rediscover it in herself by allowing herself time to come to terms with her feelings of failure and loss. She can then begin to see her past relationships in terms of gain as well as loss. She realizes the qualities she discovered in herself through relating to someone else have given her a greater sense of her own identity: she doesn't have to depend on being in love to feel a sense of wholeness in herself.

Do you know your own boundaries? Do you know who you are and who you are not? Psychologists place great importance on what they call 'boundaries', because only by knowing her boundaries can a woman know her real self.

Imagine the shape of your body. Now trace a line around that gives an extra definition to your shape. That line is your boundary that separates you from everyone else. Having this imaginary boundary around yourself means that the qualities you possess feel contained inside it. By having a boundary, you can recognise what thoughts and feelings are your own, instead of depending on others reactions for an impression of yourself. Within you own boundary, you can give shape and definition to your personality, so you feel and are seen to be a person in your own right. You know where you begin and where you end. In other words, you recognize your own limitations, but within those, you are able to develop your real qualities.

Having boundaries does not mean always surrounding yourself with layers of protection, like the thorn bushes around Sleeping Beauty's castle which prevented her suitors from getting close to her. What you need is a firm, but flexible boundary line, which separates you from others yet does not hide or disguise your real self.

Being aware of your boundaries means you feel safer about letting your partner get close to you. Instead of feeling he might take you over or move in on you without your permission, you have made a conscious decision to let him cross a boundary that normally separates you from other people. You have allowed him to know your real self.

In love-making, you can let go sufficiently to experience the closeness of feeling merged with your lover, without fearing that you might lose touch with your own identity. You have defined your own shape – your identity – which you won't lose touch with, however close and intimate the two of you become.

Test your own boundaries:

- Do you find yourself easily persuaded by your partner's opinions or point of view?
- Do you find your enthusiasm for doing something you have carefully planned, collapses if your partner opposes the idea?
- Do you find it difficult to define your own feelings – or do they feel mixed up or merged with your partner's?
- Do you find it hard to make any impression when you express your feelings? Can you make yourself 'felt'?
- Do you avoid confrontations for fear of not being able to 'hold on' to what you really want to say?
- Do you feel dependent on your partner's attitude towards you for how you feel towards yourself?
- Do you avoid real closeness with him for fear of being hurt or misunderstood?
- Do you find it hard to imagine yourself as a separate person from your partner?

If the answer to the majority of these questions is 'yes', you need to create firmer boundaries. Here's an exercise to help.

Imagine your real self, the part of yourself that contains your most vulnerable feelings, as a small circle. It may be helpful to draw your Self circle in the centre of a piece of paper.

Now imagine three circles encompassing that small, central circle. The outermost circle is your 'social' circle, where you relate to acquaintances at work or in your social life. The next circle is your 'close' circle, the one where you relate to your close friends and family. The third circle, the one that surrounds your inner, Self circle, is your 'intimate' circle, which is where you keep your most intimate and vulnerable feelings. It is the one closest to the real you.

Each circle is divided by a line; these are your boundary lines. When you first meet someone, you relate to them in your 'social' circle. If you start having a relationship, you move into your 'close' circle with the potential for allowing your partner into your 'intimate' circle.

Think about each of those circles. Do you feel able to maintain the boundaries between each one? For example, can you keep people in your social circle? Or do you find your 'close' circle invaded by acquaintances, who, if you had the choice, you would not want to get that close to you? Are you able to maintain a firm boundary line between your 'close' and 'intimate' circle? For example, do you find family or friends trying to interfere with your life or demanding too much from you? Do you find yourself invaded by others so you have no control over how close they get to you?

Now look at your relationship in terms of the spaces between each circle. In which space do you feel most comfortable with your partner? Have you become so emotionally distant that you could be relating to him in your 'social' circle? Or do you remain stuck in your 'close' circle, without feeling able to risk real intimacy?

This exercise is intended to give a structure to help you feel more in touch with your own identity – your own thoughts and feelings – by being more aware and in control of how close you allow other people to get to you.

Whichever circle you are in when you relate to someone else, you need to keep in touch with your inner, Self circle, so you remain in contact with your real feelings. Then you will find it easier to stand up for what you want from a relationship, rather than feeling overwhelmed, taken over or wiped out by the demands others make on you.

Keeping hold of a sense of your own identity makes it safer to allow more closeness in a relationship because you feel more in control of the degree of intimacy you are prepared to allow. You can stand up for yourself more easily when you keep in touch with your own feelings, because you know who you are standing up for. You give weight and substance to your feelings by staying in touch with how you really feel.

Finding out in which space you relate to your partner also can be a guide to how much intimacy you have achieved in your relationship. It can help you discover why you find it hard to let your lover cross the boundary line you put up between closeness and knowing your real self.

Lydia, 33, found herself 'taken over' by her partner in their relationship. When they decided to live together, they talked about how they would furnish their flat and what colour schemes they wanted. But somehow, it ended up looking more like his home than hers.

Lydia found it increasingly difficult to stand up for herself. Her own attitudes and opinions always seemed to collapse in any discussion or argument with her partner. When choices needed to be made, she found herself backing down and accepting his decisions because she had been persuaded that he really did know best. If she tried to talk to him about her problems, he'd somehow make her feel she was making a fuss over nothing. She never felt confident enough to really let go and make herself 'felt'.

Lydia found it difficult to hold onto any sense of her own identity in the relationship. She felt suffocated by her partner's personality. The only way she could protect herself was to withdraw inwardly and keep her most vulnerable feelings to herself. She was rarely able to let go and experience her own pleasure when she and her partner made love because she was afraid of losing all sense of herself.

Lydia had been an attractive, intelligent child, who had done well at school. Her looks and friendly personality helped her to get what she wanted and she grew up imagining that her life would always be like that. Her parents were proud of her, but they tended to spoil her and let her have her own way. At the same time, Lydia always felt she had to be a good child and not upset her parents. Her mother's health was fragile and Lydia was afraid that if she didn't behave herself, she would be too much for her mother and make her ill. Her parents were also overprotective. Whenever they had a row, Lydia was sent outside to play. When her grandmother died, she was sent away to stay with friends. She returned home to find a new bicycle waiting for her to take her mind off the loss.

Lydia's upbringing made it difficult for her to have a sense of her own boundaries. On the one hand, her parents' exaggerated her academic achievements, so she grew up imagining she could accomplish more than she was capable of. She was also never helped to come to terms with her real feelings. She tried to take her mind off any experience that was painful or unpleasant by buying herself a new dress or planning her next holiday.

Lydia found it difficult to strike a balance between closeness and distance in her relationship. Being afraid of expressing her real feelings, she felt too vulnerable if she allowed her partner to get too close. The only way she could keep her own boundaries was to distance herself emotionally from him.

Standing up for what she wanted would have given Lydia a sense of her own identity. But her fear of confrontation allowed her partner to dominate her, so she ended up not knowing which of her feelings were his and which belonged to her.

Yet even though Lydia appeared to accept his dominance, inwardly she clung to a feeling of superiority. She was secretly pleased when he got things wrong or made mistakes. It was her way of getting her own back on him. She was still hanging onto an image of herself from childhood, in which she kept an exaggerated sense of her own abilities to protect herself from facing her limitations and the more vulnerable side of her nature.

Only by getting a more balanced sense of her strengths and weaknesses could Lydia discover her real qualities. She needed to recognize her limitations so that, within those, she could begin to develop her real abilities. She would then be able to achieve a more equal partnership with her lover, instead of losing a sense of her own identity when she was with him.

When a woman falls in love, she feels intensely vulnerable. What if this relationship doesn't last? How can she cope with losing someone who matters so much to her?

It is natural to feel the need to protect ourselves against rejection and loss. But it is also important to get those fears in proportion if we are to be able to achieve real closeness in a relationship. If we are constantly afraid of becoming too emotionally vulnerable in case the relationship does not last, we limit our ability to get to know and understand both our partner and ourselves in a deeper way. Real intimacy requires a willingness to share our most vulnerable feelings, the ones we are most afraid of revealing about ourselves. It is not being prepared to break through the layers of protection we normally wrap around ourselves that keeps us from experiencing a more fulfilling kind of relationship.

The Sleeping Beauty woman finds it so hard to believe she can be loved for herself that her underlying fear is that her partner will leave her. Rather than face her fears, she is likely to find ways of trying to protect herself from losing him. Her aim is to control her lover. She only feels confident when she feels she has enough power over him to keep him.

The power of sex is one way a woman tries to possess her partner. Her aim is to remain so sexually desirable that she won't lose him. She wants her partner to need her more than she appears to need him. He has to be the one who feels vulnerable and afraid of losing her. Pleasing her partner becomes more important than her own enjoyment and satisfaction. Her own sexual feelings are aroused by seeing how much he desires her. But the more powerful she feels, the more resentful she becomes about putting his needs before her own. It is as if she's got her partner where she wants him, but that still does not satisfy her. She blames him for being selfish and self-centred, without recognizing the part she has played in encouraging him to be that way. She yearns for a more equally balanced relationship in which she feels enough trust to be herself and show her real feelings. But she's afraid that if she becomes vulnerable to her partner and shows how much she needs him, he will have too much power to hurt her.

Another way a woman tries to gain power in a relationship is by feeling she is in control of her partner's life. She gets anxious when he is out of her sight. She has to know exactly where he is and what he's been up to. She always wants to know what he's thinking or feeling. She gets upset or even ill if she feels she's not got him where she wants him.

But however devoted she may be towards the man in her life, her behaviour also disguises a clinging, possessive attitude towards him. She can't bear any uncertainty about his feelings for her or their relationship. Her own doubts and insecurities make her afraid of letting him have the freedom to be himself. She wants them to share the same interests, opinions and even feelings. She tries to ignore any differences by smoothing over any areas of conflict between them. She often doesn't 'hear' her partner when he says something that might disturb or upset their relationship, which would raise her fears of losing him.

Appearing independent is another way the Sleeping Beauty woman protects herself against her fear of losing her partner. She is the one he relies on, while she claims she could more easily manage without him. She wants her partner to depend on her, however much she inwardly resents having to carry more than her fair share of responsibility for the relationship. What she is constantly protecting herself against is her own fear of loss if she allowed herself to feel how much she really did need him.

Meg, 27, knew she was angry with her father for abandoning

her. She had been five years' old when her parents divorced. And although she had continued to see her father regularly afterwards, he was often unreliable, forgetting to 'phone her when he had promised or cancelling outings with her at the last minute because he was busy at work.

Like many children, Meg had imagined that she was somehow to blame for her parents' divorce. If she had been a more lovable little girl, her father wouldn't have left her and her mother.

Whenever she saw him, she always tried her best to be the kind of daughter she imagined he could love. She was too terrified of him cutting her out of his life completely to even allow herself to recognize the anger and hurt she had hidden when he left her.

In her relationships, Meg became possessive and clinging with her partner. She played the part of the 'little woman', who allowed her man to make the decisions and behave as if he was her big, strong protector. Outwardly, it appeared as if he was the one who controlled the relationship, but Meg kept a hold over him by working hard at making him happy. She tried to make herself indispensable to him, so, unlike her father, her partner would never leave her.

Yet in other areas of her life, Meg was a very different sort of woman. She had a responsible, well-paid job in publishing. At work, she enjoyed supervising her staff and making her own decisions. She was far from being the clinging, anxious-to-please woman she became when she fell in love. The conflict between these two aspects of herself always surfaced when the initial passion in a relationship began to wear off. Then Meg began to resent her subservient position. She felt angry that she had such a desperate need to please her partner in order to keep him. She began to accuse him of 'using' her and not caring about her feelings.

Inwardly, Meg had been left with such a fear of rejection that she did not really believe that any man would stay with her. Rather than face those fears, when problems surfaced in a relationship, she always tried to be the one who ended it. She needed to feel in control of the ending, so she did not have to experience being caught unawares by her partner walking out on her, as she had been when her father left.

How close are you and your partner? Have the two of you

achieved real intimacy? Becoming aware of how much emotional space there is between you and your partner is a guide to how close you really are.

In every relationship, there are likely to be times when a couple become so close that they feel 'as one'. Yet when differences arise between them, they can suddenly feel 'miles apart'. Going from one extreme to the other causes problems in a relationship when no middle ground has been established in which a couple can stay close enough to sort their differences out. Wanting to be too 'close' to your partner all the time means that no space is allowed between you to enable you to see your differences in a more detached and rational way. Staying too far apart means that you feel emotionally disconnected from your partner. You are isolated and out of touch with each other's feelings; you start to imagine what each other might be feeling, which is likely to make you feel even further apart.

This exercise can help measure how much closeness there is in your relationship.

Visualize the two of you sitting opposite each other about to talk over a problem in your relationship. Now look at how much space there is between you.

Physical space represents emotional distance. What's important is to get a distance between the two of you that feels right. Are you sitting close enough to touch each other? Or are you chairs wide apart?

For instance, sitting right up close to your partner so there is no space between you may feel as uncomfortable as if your chairs appear miles apart. Being too close can make you feel trapped, suffocated or completely merged with your partner. Too much distance leaves you feeling isolated and alone.

Now imagine the two of you sitting within touching distance of each other. There's a space between you, but you can still hold out your hands across that space.

Keeping in touching distance allows a couple to remain emotionally connected, while at the same time there is enough space between the two of you to also be in touch with yourself as a separate person with different needs and feelings to your partner. Feeling separate enables you to give shape and meaning to your own feelings, instead of feeling so emotionally enmeshed with your partner that you don't know which feelings are his and which are yours.

Creating this sense of being in touching distance can help you to risk more intimacy in your relationship. Because you have established yourself as a separate person, you can become vulnerable to your partner without the fear of being taken over by his personality and losing any sense of your real self. When differences arise, you can step back into your own space so you can sort out your own thoughts and feelings. Yet you also remain within touching distance of him, so you stay in touch with his feelings as well.

It is in the space between the two of you that your differences can be sorted out. Similarly, if a problem arises in the relationship that distances you from each other, you may feel so far apart from your partner that you can't sort your differences out. Being able to visualize being within touching distance in a relationship is a way of becoming in touch with each other again.

At first, you may not feel you want to get that close to each other, but you are prepared to risk moving a bit closer together. The closer you get, the more connected you become with each other's feelings. You can begin to re-establish a bond of understanding between yourself and your partner so you gradually feel able to be in touch with each other again.

Staying within touching distance of each other, you can respond to your partner's feelings because you are close enough for him to have an emotional impact on you. You can experience what he is feeling, which enables you to respond to him with more understanding.

Jane, 31, never got over losing her first lover. She had clung onto him for five years, even though he had been unfaithful during their relationship. He was such a charmer that Jane always forgave him for his other affairs. He always came back to her, telling her that she was the one woman he really cared about and pleading with her to give him a second chance. After these reconciliations, Jane's boyfriend would seem so loving and devoted to her that he could hardly bear her out of his sight. Then, a few months later, he would start to 'cool' and she'd realize that he was seeing someone else. Yet Jane was so terrified of being on her own that she was only able to give him up when another man fell in love with her.

Her new boyfriend seemed the opposite of her first lover. He appeared a steady, reliable man, who found it difficult to express his feelings. Although attracted to her, he was too emotionally withdrawn to be a passionate lover. But after her previous experience, Jane felt she had at last found the kind of safe, secure relationship she wanted.

But it didn't take long before Jane was regretting having left her former lover. The lack of sexual excitement in her new relationship and her partner's inability to share his feelings with her made her yearn for the kind of passion she had had with her other boyfriend. In her fantasies about still being with him, she 'forgot' about the other women in his life.

Jane had grown up in a family where emotions were kept under a very tight rein. Looking back, she could not even remember her parents ever cuddling or kissing each other, in front of their children. A peck on the cheek was all she had given her strict and somewhat intimidating father all her life.

Coming from such a cold and emotionally repressed background, it was no wonder that Jane longed for closeness in her relationships. Yet her yearning for emotional intimacy was outweighed by her fear of losing what she wanted most. It was that fear which attracted her to partners who, in their different ways, were equally afraid of becoming close to her. In her first relationship, Jane mistook sexual passion for real intimacy. Sex gave her the physical warmth that she had missed in her childhood, but she had picked a lover who protected himself from emotional involvement by his promiscuity. Whenever he felt 'threatened' by real feelings towards Jane, he was off with someone else.

Her second partner was similar to her own father, which gave her a sense of security but no emotional warmth. But Jane sensed that he was a man with a great deal of emotional vulnerability, which he might have been able to express in their relationship if she had tried harder to become closer to him. Jane never gave the relationship a real chance. She kept an emotional distance from her partner by comparing him unfavourably with her former lover. Even though her former partner had let her down, she preserved him in her imagination as the 'perfect' lover as a protection against putting her whole self into her next relationship. She had chosen two men who could not give her the emotional closeness she wanted but feared too much.

Her happiness was clearly apparent. She had no guilt about

being helpless and dependent on others. She had always loved to give, but she seemed at last to accept that she could now only receive. Perhaps she realized she could only give by taking – with gratitude and without guilt. Her needs were fulfilled without question and without resentment. In return she lavished praise on everyone who served her and did so with humility. Perhaps it was the first time in her life that she didn't feel she had to live up to someone else's expectations of behaviour or achievement.

Absorbed in the most difficult task of her life, that of dying, she had no doubts left.

This extract from a book *A Way To Die* (Sphere Books), describes in her parents' words how a 25-year-old girl, Jane Zorza, approached her death from cancer, which was no more than 24 hours away. In the last days of her life this young girl, who had everything to live for, had overcome her fear of dying and discovered a happiness and contentment that she had never experienced before.

She had let go of trying to please or to do what was expected of her. She was no longer trying to protect herself from the painful reality of loss that exists in all our lives. And, in doing so, she was able to accept and enjoy the love that her family and the staff in the hospice where she died had to give her. 'The world is very beautiful', she told her father, shortly before her death.

Jane's experience is by no means unique. Many people who know they have not long to live describe how that knowledge freed them to experience life more passionately and intensely. First, they had to go through a process of mourning their impending death. They would live through stages of denial, then anger, followed by the grief and pain of parting from those they loved. Yet once those feelings were overcome, they had set themselves free from the fear of loss.

Being able to accept loss as an inevitable part of life is what can transform our relationships. Then we are able to love and receive love without being so afraid of giving too much of ourselves in case the relationship does not last. We are not always counting the cost. We are free to experience what life has to offer.

It's not easy. Fear of loss goes back to the beginning of our lives and we can spend a lifetime in the futile task of trying to protect ourselves from experiencing it. The experience of loss can also have a cumulative effect. Each time we lose someone who matters to us, we tend to cut ourselves off from our more vulnerable feelings. We become more cautious and emotionally withholding in our next relationship. Because we give less of our real selves, the relationship is likely to have less chance of succeeding. Learning to cope with loss is part of growing up emotionally. It becomes easier once we become more aware of how much the fear of loss can affect and inhibit our lives.

When a relationship that matters ends, we need to go through a mourning process. We need to allow ourselves space to experience the feelings of losing someone we cared about. By not trying to deny our feelings, we find that we become less afraid of experiencing them. And, gradually, they become more bearable. By surviving what we feared most would happen to us, we become less afraid of loss in the future. We have gained the emotional strength to risk sharing our life with someone else. We have set ourselves free to love again because we have faced loss and gained maturity from the experience.

Some questions

- Think about the major losses in your life.

    Now look at ways you may have 'escaped' mourning those losses. Look at how your fear of loss may be affecting your current relationship.

- How was loss dealt with in your childhood? Were you able to express your feelings to your parents and feel that they understood? Or did you have to keep such feelings to yourself?

- What triggers feelings of loss in your life? Do you weep at a sad film or cry over a tragedy in someone else's life?

    Link those feelings to experiences of loss in your own life and allow yourself to grieve.

    Then look at what those relationships gave you. See how the qualities that the person you lost brought out in you can be brought to life again in your present life.

- Look at ways you may be trying to control your partner. Do you want him to appear to need you more than you need him?

    Reverse the situation and see what it is you fear that makes you deny your dependence on him.

- Do you put your partner's enjoyment first in love-making? How important is it to please him sexually?

What's stopping you just letting go and just experiencing your own enjoyment when you make love?

- How possessive are you with your partner? Is your dependence on him obvious or do you hold on to him in subtler ways?

  Have you enough trust in yourself and his feelings for you to let go and allow him the freedom to be himself?

- In your relationship, does one of you appear more dependent and the other more independent?

  Think of ways you could adjust that balance by accepting your dependence on each other as well as your ability to be separate individuals, each with your own identities. Look at the times when you have valued your dependence on each other. Then examine the aspects of yourself that give you an independence and an individuality that is separate from your partner.

  How much do you value each other's individuality? Does that individuality enhance your relationship or does it feel like a threat?

5
Falling for the Wrong Man

Are you the type of woman who usually has to compete with a rival for your man's love? The Sleeping Beauty woman often finds there is always someone or something in her partner's life that threatens her relationship. Sometimes it is another woman, but it may also be his job or an interest in his life that he appears much more bound up in than her.

Yet even though she feels angry and upset that she comes second in her partner's life, this kind of woman may also have a need for a rival she can constantly struggle to triumph over. She can find it becomes almost a habit for her to fall in love with a married man or someone who is already in a relationship. She feels herself strangely attracted to the need to try and 'win' him from someone else. She may find herself in the position of 'the other woman', who never quite accepts that her lover won't leave his wife and that she will always be second best.

Then there's the type who is only attracted to workaholics. Once the 'honeymoon period' in their relationship is over, he reverts to being more married to his job than to her. His work is as much of a rival as a mistress.

When a woman is usually attracted to impossible men, who cannot give her the kind of relationship she wants, she is likely to be replaying a relationship pattern that she did not overcome in childhood. She is still trying to win her father's love.

'When I grow up, I'm going to marry daddy', a little girl announces.

'No, you can't do that, dear', her mother replies with a smile. 'Daddy's already married to me.'

But however much a child may know that in reality, in her fantasy world she has a different idea. Being 'in love' with her father is a natural part of a child's psychological development. She needs the impetus of these powerful feelings towards him to discover her own femininity. Her ability to relate to her partners in adult life is to a large extent formed by her experience of this intense relationship with her father, the first and most important man in her early life.

'Winning' daddy from mother is also a child's secret, which she does not fully recognize in herself. As a small child, she won't hide her adoration of this 'hero' figure in her life. But the older she gets, she becomes guilty about her secret wishes, so she represses her feelings for her father, which then appear in disguised forms. Her crushes on hero figures such as film and pop stars, are a normal part of growing up. They give her a safe focus for her emerging sexuality without her experiencing a physical relationship before she is sufficiently mature. But hidden in her fantasies are her feelings for her father, which she still needs to overcome. What these fantasy figures also represent are unobtainable men.

However much a daughter loves her mother, she will also see her as a rival for her father's love. In a child's eyes, her mother has many of the things she wants but has to wait until she is grown up to get. Her envy of her mother is what she needs to master so she can separate emotionally from her parents and build her own life.

It is also natural for a mother to envy her daughter. As she grows up, her mother can feel envious of her youth, her looks and the potential that she has to make more of her life than her mother feels she has of her own. She has opportunities awaiting her that have passed her mother by.

If a mother is aware of her rivalrous feelings towards her daughter, she can contain them so that they do not damage the relationship. But if she fails to recognize her own envy, it is likely to undermine her attitude towards her daughter. Instead of giving her daughter confidence and encouragement in her struggle to grow up, she may try to keep her a child. Mother knows best becomes her motto. She becomes critical of her daughter's appearance, her boyfriends and any signs that she is maturing into a woman capable of making up her own mind. She may undermine her daughter's opinions and set out to make her look childish when she is trying so hard to appear grown-up.

She tells herself that she is just being protective towards her 'little girl', whom she regards as trying to grow up in too much of a hurry. Hidden within that protectiveness is likely to be the envy of a woman who does not want to face her rivalry towards the woman her daughter is becoming.

A daughter cannot avoid her mother's envy, but as she gets older, she can become more aware of the underlying rivalry between herself and her mother and how much of her own envy has a part in that. She needs to get her feelings about both her parents into proportion and to do that, she needs their help.

As a girl grows up, she often hides her envy of her mother by imagining that she is her father's favourite, the one he secretly prefers. She stages arguments to try and split her parents' allegiance to each other, so she can feel she's 'won' her father by getting him on her side. She tries to get her father's attention, so she can feel her mother is excluded from this 'special' relationship she wants to have with him. She will provoke situations where she expects him to support her against her mother, and then ends up being furious and disappointed when he does not oblige.

What a girl needs is a father who will resist treating her as his favourite and who clearly puts his wife first in his life. She has to have her hidden childhood fantasy of wanting to be daddy's 'wife' shattered, so she can move on to find fulfilment in her own relationships. It is losing her illusions about her father that helps a young girl to separate from her childhood and start the search for a partner of her own. She may be furious and disappointed with her father for not being the man she imagined. For a time, she will feel that he has really let her down. But, in fact, he has not failed his daughter. He has freed her from the need to go on competing in her adult life with a rival for her partner's love.

In Sleeping Beauty, the king bans all the spinning wheels in his kingdom in an attempt to prevent his daughter from pricking her finger. Not wanting to lose his daughter, he goes to great lengths to try and stop her from growing up. It is also significant that in the marriage service the bride's father 'gives' his daughter away. What this represents is an acceptance by the father that he must now relinquish his position as the central male figure in his daughter's life. He stands aside to allow his daughter to share her life with the man of her choice.

But a father, if he is honest with himself, finds it a struggle to let go of his little girl and accept her growing up. He remembers only too clearly the time when he was her hero and could do no wrong in her adoring eyes. It comes as a real shock when he finds that his devoted little daughter has turned into a teenager who seems totally obsessed with boys. Instead of standing back and encouraging her to become more independent, his temptation is to try to hang onto the control he has always exercised over her life. He becomes critical of her boyfriends. No one is ever good enough for his daughter. Boys, he warns her, are only after one thing. He can't sleep when she's out late and even sits up waiting until she gets home. When a boyfriend lets her down, he gives the impression that it was what he had expected all along. The message is that other men will never love his daughter as much as he does.

A young girl is likely to have mixed feelings about her father's possessiveness. She wants to grow up and become independent, so she rebels angrily against his interference in her life. Yet another part of herself secretly enjoys her father's envy of her boyfriends. In terms of her childhood struggle to compete with her mother for father's attention, she imagines she is winning hands down.

This fantasy is harder to give up if there are already problems in her parents' marriage. A teenager can feel she is her father's favourite if her parents don't appear to get on. She imagines that her father is bound to prefer his lively, attractive young daughter to what she sees as his duller, middle-aged wife. She is likely to become critical of her mother. She exaggerates or distorts what she sees as her mother's shortcomings to prove to herself that her father prefers her. At the same time, she is filled with guilt for having such bad feelings towards her mother, whom she also loves. Inwardly she is scared that she really might be able to come between her parents and even break their marriage up. She needs her parents to be a couple who won't let their daughter come between them.

No woman is ever entirely free of the feelings that accompanied her childhood struggle to be first in her father's life. In every love relationship, there is always envy about someone or something that claims too much of her partner's attention, just as she was once so envious that her mother's claim on her father came first. It is when she has not sufficiently overcome those rivalrous feelings in her childhood that her struggle to be father's favourite is repeated in her adult relationships.

Being the 'other woman' in a man's life is one of the most common ways in which this unresolved childhood conflict continues to be played out. As the mistress, a woman feels herself to be the 'special' one, the woman her lover prefers to be with, even if he still goes home every night to his wife. She needs to feel she is the one who is envied, so she doesn't have to face her own envious feelings about his wife. Yet however much her lover tells her he loves her and wants her to be first in his life, part of her is afraid of that actually happening. It is as if the intensity and excitement of the relationship depends on her having a rival, just as she once treated her mother as her rival for her father's love. At the same time, she is secretly scared of what might happen if she did become first in her lover's life.

A young girl can get caught in a trap when she becomes critical of her mother and compares her unfavourably to herself. Because of her youth, she sees herself as being more attractive and desirable than her mother. She enjoys the power of being able to twist her father round her little finger and being able to get his attention in a flirtatious, girlish way. But by doing that, she grows up with a lot of confusion about becoming a woman. She is secretly afraid of becoming a woman because of the unattractive image of womanhood her mother presents to her. Instead, she goes on playing the role of a seductive young girl in her adult relationships to stay in first place in her partner's life. What she finds difficult is becoming a woman who is mature enough to have an equal partnership with a man.

In every relationship, we see the other person not only as they are in reality, but also as projections of ourselves. We project onto them aspects of our own personalities, so they represent both our 'good' and 'bad' qualities. When a child idealizes her father and puts her mother down, she splits her 'good' and 'bad' feelings between her parents. She grows up needing to have a man to take over from her father and reflect the good feelings she has about herself. But without that masculine attention and admiration, she is likely to feel as unattractive and uninteresting as she made her mother out to be.

In her relationships, she feels confident so long as she feels desired by her partner. But when the initial passion begins to fade, she feels herself losing that power over him. She becomes afraid that he will lose interest in her and even begin to see her as the kind of woman she imagined her mother was. In repeating her childhood rivalry with her mother, she can imagine the wife or the other woman in his life to be the unattractive, uninteresting partner, which enables her to feel she is the one her lover really cares about.

Relationships are complex. There are many reasons why we are attracted to a particular man. But when a woman finds herself in the role of the 'other woman' in her partner's life, the need to repeat this childhood pattern is likely to be the dominant one. She is unconsciously repeating this experience to get a conscious understanding of her rivalrous feelings towards her mother, which prevent her from maturing into a woman who is able to have a real partnership with a man.

That is not to say that falling in love with a man who already has a partner is doomed to failure. The potential for a lasting and loving partnership may exist within the relationship. Only when the need for a rival for her partner's love has been overcome can a woman discover whether she and her partner still have a genuine attraction towards each other.

Maggie, 27, found it hard to get over a long relationship with a successful City broker who was also a married man. He had not given her the old line that he was unhappily married. But his relationship had lost the sexual intensity and excitement, which he recaptured in his affair with Maggie.

Maggie swung from feeling passionately in love to being overwhelmed by guilt and despair whenever her lover returned home to his wife. When she was rational about it, she knew that he would never leave his wife, yet that still did not stop her from constantly trying to change his mind.

She did all she could to make herself desirable to her lover. She bought herself expensive, sexy lingerie and spent the time in between seeing him planning their next evening together. Her flat was always filled with flowers for his visits. She learnt to cook his favourite meals and chose the wine carefully. She lit scented candles and played all the right music for lovers. She wanted to become so irresistible that her lover would not be able to leave her. Each time he got up and said that he had to go home, she felt a sense of failure and disappointment.

When Maggie looks back on her relationship, she can now see how unreal it was. She was constantly trying to come first in her lover's life by acting the part of a sexually desirable and constantly pleasing woman. She felt a sense of triumph over his wife when he described the noisy, chaotic mess that he went home to when his two young children were around. She imagined his wife without make up, her nails unvarnished, looking worn out and dowdy, just as her own mother had often done. It was the shock of unexpectedly seeing her lover out with his wife that brought about the end of their relationship. Maggie could not believe how different his wife was to the image she had had of her. She couldn't stop thinking about how attractive, in a quiet, understated way she had appeared and, by her attitude towards him, how close her relationship had seemed with her husband.

After that, Maggie felt used every time she saw her lover. She felt angry and humiliated by having tried so hard to make everything so perfect for a man who, as she had seen with her own eyes, was very much married to his wife.

When Maggie thought about her childhood, she realized that her father had been a similar type of man to her married lover. He had also been a successful businessman, who was not often around when she was a child. When he was there, it felt to Maggie as if the whole house was lit up with his presence. She felt herself coming to life when she heard his key in the front door.

Maggie saw her mother very differently. She appeared more concerned with trivial, household problems and nagging Maggie about her manners. Having a daughter who was a credit to her was what seemed to matter most. Maggie loved and trusted her mother, but was also angry with her for not accepting her for who she was. She felt her mother never bothered to understand her feelings, whereas she was convinced her father knew her real self. Maggie vowed that she would be nothing like her mother when she grew up. She imagined how much more exciting her father's life was. When she became a teenager, Maggie could hardly wait to get her first job and feel herself part of her father's world.

As a child, Maggie sensed there were problems in her parents' marriage. She overheard quarrels when her father was at home, when her mother would complain loudly about his absences. On one or two occasions, he had left the house after a row. Maggie heard the front door slam shut and lay in bed wondering whether her father would ever return. Yet he seemed a different person when he was with her. He was full of jokes and they laughed a lot. She remembers after hearing him quarrelling with her mother, how he had come upstairs, put his arms around her and said 'I've come to see my favourite girl'.

Inwardly, Maggie blamed her mother for her father's absences. It was she who stood in the way of him not being home more often to spend time with his 'favourite girl'. As she got older, she always made a big fuss of her father when he was at home. It wasn't hard to get his attention and he always seemed to enjoy her company. Maggie secretly believed she was the reason he had stayed with her mother.

But when Maggie looked at the snapshots in her family's photo album, she saw that the pictures told a different story. Her childhood memory had been selective and only allowed her to remember what fitted her fantasy about her parents' marriage. In the album, there were pictures of her parents with their arms around each other, of them laughing and having fun. Whatever their problems, there had been a closeness between them. They looked a real couple, just as Maggie's married lover and his wife had seemed.

By realizing this, Maggie was finally able to let go of her childhood rivalry with her mother and accept that, despite the difficulties in their marriage, she had come first in her husband's life. As a child, Maggie had blamed her mother for causing her father's absences to protect herself from feeling angry with her father for his neglect of his family. Her fantasies about being first in his life had prevented her from realizing how much his absences hurt her and how lonely and neglected he made her feel. In reality, Maggie had never felt certain enough of father's love to show him how she really felt. Her relationship with a married man had been a repeat of that relationship with her father. She had put herself in the position of the other woman because of her underlying fear that she was not capable of coming first in any man's life.

By getting a more realistic picture of her parents, Maggie began to lose her fear of becoming a woman like her mother. When she no longer put her father on a pedestal, she found she could appreciate more of her mother's good qualities. She was able to get her feelings about both her parents more in proportion and realize they had both loved her in their own way. In coming to terms with her relationship with her parents, Maggie set herself free from her need to repeat her childhood rivalry with her mother in her adult relationships. She began to believe that she could have a relationship in which she came first in her partner's life.

Being attracted to 'eternal triangle' relationships is a pattern that starts in childhood. A child can feel so caught up in her parents' relationship that it is almost as if she's the one who keeps their marriage together.

A young girl may sense that her mother is using her to hang on to her father. The feeling she gets is that he only stays because of his children. This creates a dilemma for a teenager. She wants to keep her parents together, but she also wants to be free to live her own life. Instead she feels expected to remain the go-between in their marriage. She can get so caught up in her parents' problems that she puts off sorting out her own conflicting feelings about growing up.

Childhood conflicts that don't get sorted out at the time emerge in our adult relationships. We can find ourselves constantly attracted to men whose emotional development got stuck at the same stage in childhood as our own. Our partners reflect some of the same problems as we had about growing up.

Tania, 29, finds that all the men she'd been seriously involved with had one thing in common: they were their mother's favourite sons. In the relationship that meant most to her, her partner's mother not only seemed like her rival, but she also tried to treat Tania as the 'other woman' in her son's life. She was possessive about her son and envious of Tania's influence over him. Tania was the one who was blamed when her partner neglected his mother or was irritable or moody when he visited her.

Tania's relationship contained the elements of her own childhood struggle to win her father from her mother. In this respect, her partner represented her father, while she saw his mother as her rival, the woman, like her own mother, who stood in the way of her being first in his life.

Her partner also had not overcome his own childhood rivalry, except he faced the problem in reverse. His need to remain a mother's boy showed that he was still caught up in rivalrous feelings towards his father about who came first in his mother's life.

Tania had always felt much closer to her father than her mother. When she was a child, her mother always encouraged her to think she was special to her dad. 'Don't upset your father. He loves you so much', this only child remembers her mother saying.

Looking back, Tania realizes that her mother may have used her daughter to help keep her marriage together. Whatever marital problems her parents had, her father was less likely to walk out if it meant also losing his daughter. Tania's father spent a great deal of time with her. Most evenings, he helped her with her homework. They would read books together, discuss their favourite TV programmes and on weekends he often took her fishing. He taught her to play tennis and swim.

Tania imagined she was like her father in all sorts of ways. They had the same eyes, the same shaped mouth and similar hands. Their tastes were similar too. They liked the same food, laughed at the same jokes and enjoyed serious discussions that she imagined went above her mother's head.

Like all daughters, Tania envied her mother for having all the things she wanted but wasn't old enough to have. Instead of facing up to those feelings, she saw her mother as the one who envied her for having such a close relationship with her father. In her fantasy, she turned her mother into someone who was excluded from the relationship she had with her dad.

When Tania was with her father, she felt good about herself. But without him, she felt there was something 'bad' and 'horrible' about her. She felt so full of envy and guilt towards her mother, that there was very little space left for Tania's loving feelings towards her. The way she felt about her mother convinced her that no one would love her if they knew what she was really like.

In some respects, Tania's father had given her a good foundation for her future relationships. She always felt at ease with men and enjoyed their company. Her father's interest in her had given her confidence in herself and her abilities. But Tania also needed to rediscover her loving feelings towards her mother so she could feel worthy of being loved for herself. Casting her mother in the inferior role in her childhood meant that Tania could deny any qualities that she regarded as inferior in herself. Yet at the same time, having such a low opinion of her mother made her feel guilty and dislike herself.

Tania was prevented from getting her feelings about both her parents in proportion by a series of family disasters when she was growing up. Her father was made redundant from his job when she was a teenager and both he and her mother became ill with the shock. 'Don't bother your father', her mother would say. 'He's not feeling well.' Tania felt cut off from both her parents, who had become much more preoccupied with their own feelings than hers. She felt she had been left to do her growing up alone.

Her involvement with a man who was at heart still a 'mother's boy' was her attempt to master her childhood rivalry with her mother. 'Winning' her partner from his mother gave Tania the same sense of superiority that she had experienced when she had tried to exclude her own mother from her relationship with her father. But instead of achieving a more mutual relationship with her partner, he then expected her to take over the role his mother had played in his life.

In her relationship, Tania had the ingredients which could help her understand and overcome her need for a rival for her partner's love. Instead of trying to exclude her partner's mother, she was able to stop competing with her and allow her an important place in her son's life. Once Tania had lost her rivalrous feelings, her partner's mother also experienced a change in her attitude. Because she no longer felt so threatened by Tania, she became less interfering in her son's relationship. It was as if she had finally accepted Tania came first in his life.

What Tania and her partner had to discover was whether they were still attracted to each other after their need to replay this triangular relationship had lost its power over both of them. Without the drive to win her partner from his mother, Tania had to find out whether they shared other, more positive qualities that would help them to turn their relationship into a more grown-up and fulfilling love affair.

A woman whose father was a remote or absent figure in her childhood is still likely to retain a fantasy about herself being first in his life. He may have been a father who encouraged this illusion by occasionally appearing in her life with presents, declarations of love and excuses why he couldn't be the father who was always there for her. Or he may have been someone she never knew at all, so she replaced his physical presence with a fantasy about an idealized father she imagined would have put her first in his life if he had really known her.

A woman whose real father was not around enough in her childhood is likely to search for men who have certain qualities that fit the image of the father she would have liked to have had. Her anger and resentment about him not being there in her childhood may be partly directed towards her mother, whom she secretly blames for him not being around while she was growing up.

Hidden behind her inner image of an ideal father is another male figure who carries all the anger, mistrust and disappointment she feels towards her real father, which surface each time a man lets her down. She may even project her feelings about her father onto a political or ideological cause and become a passionate supporter of its aims, while being totally blind to any other point of view. Everyone who opposes what she believes in is seen as an enemy. Men are either 'goodies' or 'baddies' – heroes or villains. There is no sense of proportion about the way she feels.

When a young girl grows up without a father, it is harder for her to give up her childhood illusions. What she has missed out on is the struggle to win him from her mother, which, when lost, enables her to develop a more balanced attitude towards both her parents, so she can relate in a more realistic way to her partners in her adult life. Instead she unconsciously looks for situations in which she can experience this childhood conflict to give herself the chance to sort her feelings out.

A man in a position of power can have a fatal attraction for a woman who has inwardly remained a little girl 'in love' with father and has been searching for a man to take his place in her life. This type of man has many of the attributes of an idealized father figure. The people who work for him or are in a subservient position can be seen as rivals for his attention. So if he singles her out for his special attention, she becomes what in her childhood fantasies she dreamed of being – daddy's favourite girl. In terms of her delayed childhood struggle to 'win' father from mother, she has found rivals for his attention in the shape of his other employees or even his job, which he appears to be married to. What a woman attracted to this kind of man wants is to win over these rivals and prove to herself that she comes first in his life.

Kate, 36, found herself in love with her boss shortly after a long-term relationship had broken up. At first, Kate was devastated when her partner left her for a younger woman. She lost so much self-confidence, she couldn't even imagine herself ever attracting a man again.

Her boss at the advertising agency where she worked was sympathetic about her failed relationship. He put no pressure on her when she took time off and took care to treat her gently in the office. After working late one evening, he suggested they went out for a drink. Kate poured out her feelings and then unaccountably, she began to feel more confidence in herself. She sensed that her boss was attracted to her and she started responding to him. She felt herself coming to life again.

Kate knew her boss was married. His wife often popped into the office and she was an attractive, lively woman who was liked by the staff. Having an affair with him would have created a lot of problems at work and Kate was determined not to go that far. But she didn't see what harm a little flirtation could do. At least it could give her back her self-confidence.

It didn't take long before Kate found herself waking up

every morning and actually looking forward to going to work. She began to take a lot of trouble over her appearance. In her office, she was always waiting for her boss to come over to talk to her. He usually stayed longer chatting to her than the others and Kate felt excited when they joked and laughed together in front of the other staff. In executive meetings when they discussed their advertising accounts, he seemed to pay Kate more attention than the others and responded to her ideas with more enthusiasm.

She spent a lot of her spare time dreaming up advertising campaigns that she thought would please her boss. She liked to make some of her ideas amusing so that she could make him laugh. She imagined that she was showing him how she felt about him, but in a way that no one else on the staff would guess what was going on.

Eventually, another executive voiced the resentment that had been building up in the office. Far from Kate's flirtation not being noticed, it was the main topic of discussion between the rest of the staff. They were sick and tired, Kate was told, of her showing off to their boss. And they were fed up with all the attention she was getting in return.

Kate was devastated. Not only did she feel exposed and humiliated, but she also realized how much it had mattered to get more of her boss's attention than anyone else. Yet the reaction it had caused had made her lose that special treatment. Her boss had denied that he had been treating Kate any differently. He then made a point of not stopping by her desk for a chat. In meetings, she felt he purposely ignored her presence.

Kate's attraction to her boss had been more than a way of escaping her feelings of rejection when her lover had left her. The underlying reason lay in her childhood, when Kate's father had walked out on her mother after falling in love with a younger woman. Kate had adored her father, yet inwardly she was furious with him for having the power to hurt her so much. She was also angry with her mother for appearing 'inferior' to the woman her father had left her for.

Kate became aware that her relationship with her boss was an attempt to sort out her childhood conflicts. In her fantasy about him, he had represented her father, a powerful, yet unobtainable man. His wife, his work and his employees Kate had tried to put in an inferior position to herself so she could pretend that she came first in his life, as she had so wanted to be first in her father's affections. Putting herself in a superior position in the office had been a way of restoring her self-confidence. She had become the one who was envied, which stopped her feeling so envious of her lover's new girlfriend. What made it so much more painful was that she had never been able to overcome her childhood envy towards her father's girlfriend and her deep fear of rejection that he had left her with when he walked out.

Fortunately, Kate had reexperienced her still powerful childhood need to be first in her father's life without breaking up her boss's marriage or even losing her own job. By understanding herself better, she also began to have a less fixed image of her parents. She became more aware of them as individuals with their own psychological history and emotional conflicts, in which she had been involved, but was also separate from. She was also able to be more understanding about her father when she got her feelings about him more in proportion. She realized that his leaving his family for another woman did not have to mean that she would always find herself rejected in the same way.

Every phase in childhood is, to a greater or lesser extent, repeated in our adult relationships. Every emotional conflict that is not sorted out, reappears and, rather like an old record, gets played over and over until we have understood the underlying message that it is trying to convey.

Anger, resentment, envy and guilt are part of all close relationships. We are bound to have intense and conflicting feelings about a person we also love and care about. If we think: 'Why do I feel like this? What is my anger or my resentment really about?' we can begin to look at these feelings in a different way. Rather than allowing them to build up inwardly and then using them to attack or punish our partner, we can understand them and come to terms with them without having an unconscious need to act these feelings out.

When feelings get out of proportion, it is because they do not just relate to what is happening in our life in the present, but also to incidents from the past. Something has happened in the here and now that has connected us with powerful emotions that were repressed in childhood and have been waiting for the chance to surface in our adult lives. Not being aware of this means we constantly have the same arguments, build up the same resentments, feel envy and guilt in each of our relationships. Once we understand the connection with the past, those feelings lose their power over us. Instead of being repressed and out of our control, they become feelings we can handle and contain within ourselves. Instead of finding ourselves constantly repeating the same mistakes, we can leave the past behind and begin to experience a different kind of relationship, which is built on a real understanding of ourselves and our partner.

Some questions

- Do you secretly need a rival for your partner's love? Look at your childhood relationship with your parents. Did you idolize your father and put your mother down? Did you imagine yourself to be your father's favourite and have a special relationship with him that excluded the rest of the family?

  Now look at your adult relationships. How much is that pattern still being repeated?

- Do you always need to feel special to every man you have a relationship with? Are you never satisfied unless you feel you've become the most important person in his life?

- Do you feel much more sexual excitement with a man who is already involved in a relationship with someone else?

- Do other women seem envious of you? Are you always afraid they would think badly of you if they really knew you?

  Reverse these feelings and you are likely to find it is your own envy and 'bad' feelings towards them that you are avoiding facing in yourself.

- Do you expect a man to fulfil all your needs and make you feel protected and secure? Are you always being let down because you only imagined that he knew how you felt?

- If the answer to these questions is Yes, the influence of your childhood relationship with your parents is still having a powerful influence over your adult life.

  To change this pattern think about your image of both your parents. Is it a fixed, stereotyped image that you've carried inside you since childhood but that now needs to grow up?

  Look at your mother. Try and see her good qualities and her

failings. Then link them to what you know of her past and what she had to cope with in her married life. Can you now see a different person emerging? Has she become a real woman you can understand better and more easily forgive for sometimes letting you down? Can you get your feelings about her in proportion, so she no longer seems someone on whom you have to get your own back?

Repeat this process with your father. Try to understand him as a real-life person with his own faults and failings, as well as his good qualities.

Then picture your parents at some point in their lives when they were a real couple who put each other first.

You are inwardly uniting these images of your parents in a relationship which you were not part of. By doing that, you set yourself free to find a relationship that does not depend on competing with a rival for your partner's love.

6
Living Happily Ever After?

When Sleeping Beauty marries her prince, the fairy tale describes them as living happily ever after. Looked at symbolically, that means the princess has reached a level of maturity where she is able to form the most rewarding and challenging relationship of all – a lifelong commitment to her partner.

Every relationship we have can be a stepping stone towards achieving a 'till death us do part' partnership. Our ability to sustain a mutually satisfying marriage or long-term committed relationship depends to a great extent on how much we have learnt from past relationships, not only in terms of relating to another person, but also in discovering ourselves through relating to our former partners.

At its most fundamental level, a good marriage is based on an interdependence between two people. It means that we have the ability to recognize both our dependence on each other and our need to retain and develop our own individuality. The struggle to reconcile these opposing needs is what creates growth and change in a relationship. It is the 'marriage' of these two aspects of ourselves that helps us achieve a rewarding lifetime partnership with another person.

Marriage is a relationship which can provide the greatest potential for personal growth and maturity. In taking their wedding vows, a couple are making what they intend and hope is a permanent commitment to each other, which means that they are committing themselves to great changes in their life and personality. They are providing themselves with a structure within which they can feel secure and trusting enough to work out difficulties in past relationships. At the same time, they can also discover more of their own abilities and potential in the qualities that their partner and their marriage brings out in them.

The success of a marriage depends a great deal on our choice of partners. But how does a woman know when she has met Mr Right? How can she be sure he is the man she wants to spend the rest of her life with?

A woman's choice of a husband can be based on compatability.

'It's not just sex,' she tells her family and friends, 'we get on so well together. He's the only man I've ever felt I could actually live with.'

Sharing the same interests, tastes and ambitions is a powerful motivation for marriage. Because they seem so similar, a couple feel that they can work out the kind of life they both want. But a woman can also feel she has no such rational reasons for her choice of a lifetime partner. Instead she feels compelled by such an overwhelming desire for her partner that however different and mismatched they appear, she cannot resist marrying him. Her family and friends' warnings about the unsuitability of the marriage make no difference. 'I've never felt like this about anyone before', she explains. 'There's something magical about our feelings for each other.'

These 'magical' feelings come from the unconscious motivation in the relationship, which creates the powerful attraction between a couple. They have recognized elements in each other that match their own psychological needs and development. The magical feeling they get when they are together exists because this psychological 'fit' between them makes them feel an exhilarating sense of wholeness in themselves.

At an unconscious level, it is not only their similarities, but the differences in their psychological make-up that attracts a couple to each other. They each have what the other needs to continue their own individual process of growth. The hope is that through the personality of this person they have chosen to marry they will be able to sort out emotional difficulties, which they had not been able to do in previous relationships.

It takes confidence to go against conventional wisdom and put our trust in irrational feelings when choosing a marriage partner. How successful such marriages are depends a great deal on how much self-knowledge both partners have or are prepared to gain to enable their initial passion to grow into a deeper understanding of each other. What they may discover is that they have been attracted to each other because they shared a similar fantasy about what being married would be like. Because of this shared, inner fantasy, they were able to appear the ideal partner, the magical prince or princess each had been looking for. It is only when they see through their illusions that they begin to realize what each other is really like. Then they may be faced with the more destructive elements in each other's personalities which have been hidden behind the image which they were attracted to.

At this stage, it may seem as if they have married for all the wrong reasons or they have picked someone who is the opposite of the person they imagined was their ideal mate. But if they can get an understanding of these negative aspects in their relationship, they may find that unconsciously they have chosen the right person to marry after all. As well as being attracted to positive qualities in their partner, they have been drawn to 'weaknesses' or 'failings' that also reflect more negative aspects of their own personalities. It is as if the unconscious part of themselves is trying to make them recognize what they have to master in their own psychological make-up to discover more of their real selves. Without knowing it, they are striving for the sense of 'wholeness' that they felt fleetingly when they first fell in love.

There are always powerful unconscious motivations underlying the choice of a marriage partner. No husband is 'made to measure', however similar or compatible to his partner he appears on the surface. In her husband, a woman is likely to recognize qualities which she valued in her parents or other important people in her past. It is these similarities which help her feel confident about committing herself to her partner for life. She is also likely to be attracted to elements in her husband's personality that were lacking in previous relationships, which make her feel her marriage will enable her to make a fresh start.

For instance, she may choose a man as intelligent and able as her own father, but who is more reliable and capable of greater tenderness than her father was. Similarly, her husband may have been attracted to her because her liveliness and attractiveness reminded him of his mother, yet she appears less dominating and possessive than he had experienced his mother to be.

What may also surface are the more destructive aspects of their personalities that they both share. It is often remarkable how closely negative aspects in one partner match or are the opposite of aspects in the other partner's personality. Each has found a partner whose psychological make-up fits their own. For example, a woman who has repressed her own angry and violent feelings may marry a man who appears as easy going and compliant as herself. But, as the relationship progresses, his real temper begins to emerge, which frightens her so much that she withdraws emotionally.

What she is doing is repeating a childhood pattern in which she felt her parents withdraw whenever anger was expressed. Her fear of anger came from the occasional rages her father flew into unexpectedly. Anger seemed too destructive and terrifying to cope with, so she learnt to repress her own. In her choice of husband, she picked a man whose angry outbursts were similar to her father's rages. His own past experience was being repeated in his marriage, where he had chosen a wife like his own mother, who backed off when he became angry, so he was left with both the guilt and the frustration of his feelings not being understood. What made his temper more violent was that he was also picking up his wife's repressed anger, so he was expressing her angry feelings as well as his own. What their marriage offered was the chance for the wife to get in touch with her own anger, so she could feel a person with more inner substance, who had the strength to stand up for her own feelings. Being able to express her own anger would reduce her husband's need to express all the angry feelings in the relationship. His own anger would become more manageable, so the feelings he was expressing could be more readily understood.

Another example of a couple whose negative aspects prove a psychological fit is when the wife feels inferior to her husband who appears to possess all the self-confidence she lacks. At social gatherings, he is the one who works overtime to get attention, while she stays in the background and makes little or no impression. She is likely to be a woman who felt put down in childhood and grew up lacking any real feelings of self-worth. One of the main reasons she married her husband was that he appeared to be so assertive and had also fallen in love with the real her. She felt she had finally found a man who understood and appreciated her. But that appreciation began to fade once they were married. Then it appeared as if he was always looking for ways to put her down and make her into the inferior partner. Without realizing it, she had picked a man who was as insecure about himself as she was. His exaggerated efforts to be popular and make an impression masked his own lack of confidence. Constantly finding fault with his wife was his attempt to bolster his own lack of self-worth.

Realizing that they had been attracted to each other because they shared the same insecurities is what they needed to discover about themselves. Because she understood only too well what it was like to feel inferior, the wife could show more understanding towards her husband, so he became less afraid of facing those same feelings in himself. He would not need to try so hard to be popular. He could become more of his real self. Realizing he was not the confident, self-assured man he appeared would relieve his wife of her need to feel inferior. She could then refuse to allow him to put her down. She could begin to challenge him when he tried to point out her 'faults'. Through overcoming these negative aspects in her marriage, she would be able to find her own confidence and sense of self-worth.

Every couple knows that no marriage is perfect. They realize there are going to be conflicts between them – but what they often don't anticipate is that their weak spots, their most vulnerable feelings, are the ones most likely to feel under attack. They have chosen a partner who is likely to bring out their worst qualities, aspects of their personalities that they have hidden, even from themselves. 'He's not the same man I married', a wife says after the honeymoon period in their marriage has passed. 'Nor is she the woman I fell in love with', retorts her husband. Coping with the inevitable disappointment that their marriage has not turned out to be all each partner had expected is the first real test of their partnership.

What creates more pressure is that the couple cannot walk away from their difficulties as easily as they may have done in the past. They have signed a contract to stay together, for better or for worse. They become afraid of the emotional commitment they have made and the possibility of being let down and failing to make the marriage work. The vast majority of couples enter marriage with high expectations, which make them idealize each other's good qualities and minimize their failings. In finding someone who appears to live up to their romantic ideal, they have become caught up in the excitement of recognizing the similarities that exist between them, while ignoring or minimizing their differences.

Some marriages are not going to work out. It can happen that once a couple get to know both the worst as well as the best in each other, they realize the underlying reasons for their mutual attraction were more fantasy than reality, more destructive than constructive. They may also be unprepared to face aspects of themselves that they and their partner bring out in each other. The difference between the fantasy and what turns out to be the reality of marriage is too wide a gap to bridge.

It is a true saying that you have to work at achieving a good marriage. For a start, we don't really appreciate anything that we haven't struggled hard to achieve. And marriage or any long-term, committed relationship, being the most difficult and demanding of all partnerships, carries the best rewards if we succeed. In struggling to overcome the difficulties we are bound to face in a marriage, we give ourselves the opportunity to increase our self-knowledge. We discover a sense of fulfilment and meaning in our relationship that comes from a deepening understanding of both our partner and ourselves.

What attracted Christine to her husband Tom was that he was such an ambitious and outwardly confident man. He appeared so different from her father, who had stayed in the same, routine job for years and seemed afraid of any change or challenge in his life. As a talented young architect, Tom had the drive and the ability to take risks in his career to get where he wanted.

Tom, too, felt he had chosen a wife who was the opposite of his own mother, who had been a stay-at-home wife. Christine had qualified as a solicitor and had no intention of giving up her job when they married. In Tom's eyes she appeared a self-sufficient, independent young woman, so different from his mother who he suspected had been frustrated and bored by the subservient role she had seemed to play in his parents' marriage.

Both Christine and Tom viewed their own parents' marriages as rather dull, lifeless relationships, held together by convention and familiarity. They were convinced theirs would be different.

At first Christine and her new husband seemed the perfect couple. They were both absorbed in building a home together, which Tom designed. They spent their weekends searching for the right furnishings, bought cookery books and entertained their friends at lively dinner parties. Then, gradually, the novelty began to wear off. Their home was completed and Tom began to lose interest in it and his job as well. He decided to become a freelance architect, which would give his talents more scope but would also mean that he would have to give much more time to his work, as well as being prepared to take on projects that took him away from home. It was a risk, but one they could afford as Christine had a secure, well-paid job – and hadn't she married Tom for his adventurous spirit?

It was at this point that problems in their marriage began to surface. After her initial enthusiasm about her husband's new career had worn off, Christine started bitterly to resent his absorption in his work. Working for himself meant that he was often away and when he was at home he never kept regular hours. Yet she was the one who was expected to be at home for him. Christine had always been determined not to be like her mother, who gave up her career when she married to look after her family and had seemed resentful about her missed opportunities. Over the years, Christine had watched how lacking in self-confidence and dependent on her husband her mother had become. Christine's career had given her the independence and self-worth her mother had lacked. Yet even with her job, she found herself playing the same, subservient role in her marriage as her mother had done.

Her own career had also become an extension of her married role. She began to see her job as dull and routine compared to the exciting, creative work of designing buildings that so absorbed her husband. It was as if she was working to provide him with the security so he could afford to take the risks to achieve a successful career for himself. Yet, at the same time, he seemed to give her little in return. His job came first. He was not interested in a social life and rarely wanted to make the effort to go out in the evenings or weekends.

Christine remembered the effort her mother had made to get her husband to share a more stimulating social life, until she finally gave up and resigned herself to spending every evening sitting at home watching TV with him. She began to see her own husband as equally selfish and self-centred as her father had appeared to be.

Tom also began to feel trapped by the demands that Christine was making on him. He realized that it wasn't easy for her when so much of his energy was taken up by his work. But he felt that she should be more understanding about the demands his job made on him, instead of getting angry when he was too exhausted to take her out or because he had been too busy to 'phone and tell her what time he would be home. Tom began to feel that instead of being the self-sufficient career woman he had thought he'd married, Christine had turned out to be just as dependent, demanding and clinging as his mother had been.

Christine and her husband had been so attracted by the qualities they had admired in each other that they had not faced an underlying insecurity in both their personalities, which had also drawn them to each other. Christine's determination to have her own career showed her to be a woman with more self-confidence than her mother had possessed. But what she had never recognized in herself was her fear of being an independent, emotionally mature woman, fully capable of standing on her own feet. She had given the appearance of being that sort of woman in her job, but it was a different story in her personal life. She had always needed a relationship with a man to feel secure and protected. When each of her affairs had ended, she had always felt lost and alone until another man had come into her life. When she met Tom, he fulfilled her need for a strong, protective partner who would take risks in life for her. What she projected onto her husband was her own need to face up to the kind of challenges she was most afraid of. To Christine, becoming a freelance architect represented Tom's ability to be independent and stand on his own feet and she felt resentful and envious of his apparent ability to be what she was afraid of being herself.

But Tom was not as emotionally strong and independent as he appeared to Christine. Though talented and ambitious, he also had realized how important it had been to Christine that he could take the plunge and set himself up in what was an uncertain and insecure career. His near obsessional interest in his work masked his very real fear of failure. Inwardly, he resented having to be the risk-taker in the marriage and he punished Christine for not understanding his fears by not having the time for a social life with her.

What Christine didn't appreciate was how much her husband needed her to be there to give him the security and protection that was lacking in his job. To some extent, he needed a woman like his mother who would play the subservient role in the marriage so he could appear to be the successful, independent partner, rather than face his own hidden fears about his lack of self-confidence and self-worth.

Christine and Tom had been attracted to both similarities and differences in each other. Their appreciation of each other's abilities to achieve more in their lives than either of their parents was a strong and positive aspect of their marriage. What they had done, though, was to take on roles in their relationship which protected them from facing hidden anxieties about themselves.

Christine needed to mature and to start creating challenge and excitement in her own life. Instead of leaning on Tom's achievements, she needed to build up her own self-confidence and an inner sense of independence, which would prevent her from feeling so resentful of her dependence on her husband. By creating her own separate identity within the marriage, she would no longer have to rely on Tom to provide all the interest and stimulation in her life. By taking that pressure off her husband, she would relieve him of the need to be the successful partner, so he would then find it easier to come to terms with his own fear of failure, both in his job and his marriage.

By striking a balance between their dependence on each other and their need to develop their separate identities, Tom and Christine could start to build a real partnership, in which they could support and strengthen each other while taking a more equal responsibility for their marriage.

Initially, getting married is an awakening because it brings about such great changes in a couple's lives. The wedding, honeymoon and setting up home together all symbolize a separation from their parents and an adjustment to their new roles as husband and wife. They can get so swept along by these outward changes that it is only when all the fuss has died down and they find themselves alone together, that they realize how much they have to adjust inwardly to sharing their lives.

Another big adjustment happens in their relationship with their own families. However long it has been since they actually left home, the dependence on their parents can still have been an important, underlying factor in their lives. The fact that they have not really separated from their families may have been disguised by them having relationships before marriage in which they felt very dependent on their partners, so they have never really found their own, separate identity. Marriage becomes either a relationship where they can continue to do their growing up together or one where they fall back on old patterns of relating because they feel familiar and safe. They begin to feel as dependent on their partner as they once did on their parents, but these feelings are accompanied by resentment and anger that their marriage makes them feel trapped.

Re-creating aspects of our parents' relationship in our own marriage is inevitable. We need role models on which to base our own relationships and what we observed in our parents relationship will have a significant effect on our own. Our need may be the reverse of what we experienced in childhood. In marriage, we may look for the stability or warmth that was missing in our parents' relationship. Whereas other couples, who have benefited from a close family background, will recreate those qualities in their own marriage to build a secure and loving base.

Every marriage needs an underlying sense of security, a bond that exists between a couple so they know that they are there for each other and that they are the ones who matter most in each other's lives. Just as each partner needs to recognize both their dependence on each other and their need to develop their own individuality, so a marriage needs a strong, dependable foundation from which each of them can discover what they want from their lives.

It is change and growth brought about by understanding each other's individual and shared needs that enriches a marriage and keeps it a lively, stimulating relationship. Repeating familiar relationship patterns, smoothing over differences and backing off from experiences that would bring about change in a relationship, are ways in which a marriage loses its vitality.

Like Sleeping Beauty, a bride on her wedding day may feel she has at last found her true prince. But instead of marriage being an awakening to new possibilities in themselves, their life together becomes so safe, familiar and predictable, it is as if they have both fallen into a never-ending sleep.

Kay breathed a sigh of relief on her wedding day. Not that she wasn't frightened of the enormity of the commitment she had just made to her chosen partner for life. But there was an overwhelming sense of relief at the same time. Kay felt safe and protected. She imagined she would never feel alone again.

Six years later, Kay realized that she had not found the emotional closeness she had been looking for in marriage. In fact, she sometimes felt more lonely with her husband than she was by herself.

Kay's family background appeared stable and secure. Her parents had stayed married, her father had stayed in the same job until he retired and they still lived in the same house. Her parents rarely argued or disagreed either, so a real row was a frightening event. When that happened Kay always imagined that their family life was about to be shattered but, afterwards, her parents' differences would be smoothed over again and life would go on as if nothing had happened. Because these disagreements were never talked about, Kay grew up afraid of confrontation. She learnt to hide her real feelings, just as her parents did.

Right from when she started dating, she had wanted to marry and had become engaged twice before she actually made it to the altar. She wanted the security of marriage to give her the security to be able to express her real feelings to a partner who loved her for being herself. In her husband, Mike, she imagined she had found a man who had the assertiveness she needed to discover in herself.

Mike's own background had been the opposite of hers. His father's army career had taken the family to live in various parts of the world while Mike was growing up. It often felt as if he had only just settled down in a school and made some friends, when he would have to move again. The army life suited his parents, who liked being constantly on the move. Changing countries, making new acquaintances and leading a hectic social life made up for the lack of real closeness in their marriage. Mike found it difficult to believe that they really loved him as they had so little time for their son.

This upbringing forced him to become self-sufficient and appear more grown-up than he felt inwardly. He gave the impression of being a self-assured man with an outwardly assertive, even aggressive manner. He saw marriage to Kay as giving him the chance to gain more security and have the close, loving family life that he had missed in his unsettled childhood.

Outwardly, their marriage appeared to fulfill Mike's childhood dream. They bought a picture-book cottage and made it really cosy to live in. Although Kay kept her secretarial job, she would rush home from the office to get Mike's meal for him. She loved playing at being the 'perfect' wife as she saw how much he enjoyed her looking after him. She would bite her tongue when she'd come back home to find how much of a mess Mike had left the place in. He wanted a nice home, but he treated the cottage like a hotel with her as the maid who was expected to clean up after him. But Kay was so afraid of spoiling the image of their idyllic life together that she bottled up her resentment and got down to the housework.

Kay wanted to have a different marriage from her parents. In the early days of her marriage, she tried to confront any differences between herself and Mike, but he always reacted as if she was making a fuss over nothing and she would end up almost believing him. She wanted to keep her husband as the outwardly assertive, self-assured man she had married. She was afraid of shattering that image by exposing the weaker, more vulnerable side of his nature if she really challenged him.

Mike began to repeat his parents' unsettled pattern of life by constantly changing jobs in the advertising field where he worked. At first, he convinced Kay that these job changes were shrewd career moves, but gradually she realized that they were much more about Mike's fear of making a real commitment to anything in his life. It felt as if he had the same attitude towards his marriage. He wanted a home and a wife, yet he wasn't prepared to really commit himself to either. He was always out and about, socializing with business contacts or at the pub with friends.

Mike's problem was that he had lost so much during his childhood that he was afraid of making a real emotional commitment to Kay or to his career in case he again had to lose what he really cared about. He protected himself from his fear of loss by always being on the move and never allowing himself to feel too dependent on anyone. He needed Kay to help him overcome those fears by making him feel that he really mattered to her. But she was too angry and disappointed in her husband to give him reassurance.

Kay had wanted a strong, protective husband, so she would not have to face her fears about standing on her own feet. But when she discovered that Mike was not nearly as confident and assertive as he made himself out to be, she felt so let down and angry that she finally began to confront their differences. She challenged Mike in such an attacking way that he backed off and became even more remote and distant. Their rows became like those between her own parents – explosions of feelings that were never discussed afterwards, so they were left with no understanding of each other.

Yet Mike and Kay still had the ability to have a close and loving partnership. To do that they both needed to develop a more realistic attitude towards their 'idyllic' marriage so they could stop feeling so let down by each other. By finding her own assertiveness, Kay would feel less threatened by Mike's underlying lack of confidence. Instead of attacking him for not being the husband she had imagined, she could begin to understand and help him come to terms with his fear of commitment. Learning to love each other for their weaknesses as well as their strengths would help create a bond between them in their marriage that was based on a real knowing of themselves.

Having children is a great test of the strength of a marriage. A couple need to understand and be prepared for the adjustments that have to be made within themselves and their marriage if their partnership is to change for the better and not for the worse.

For all the joy a baby may bring to their lives, a child also demands an emotional commitment that can seem overwhelming, especially in the first year of its life. For a woman, her baby's needs can seem to take over her life completely. The sense of oneness that she and her baby experience in the early months can cause conflict within herself and in her relationship to her husband. It is a time when she may feel that apart from being a mother, she has lost touch with other aspects of her identity. While her preoccupation with her baby can make her husband feel resentful about being excluded from this special mother–child relationship in which at first he plays only a minor, supporting role.

How well a couple cope with this change in their partnership depends on how much understanding already exists between them and how secure they feel about their own identities. Then they can both more easily accept the intensity of this early mother and child bond as a phase that leads to the baby becoming more aware of itself as a separate individual, which enables its mother to recover her own identity and her role as a mutual partner in her marriage.

Childbirth, like any deeply emotional experience, connects us with feelings that go back to the beginning of our own lives. While we cannot consciously remember our own birth, the emotional impact of it remains contained in our most vulnerable feelings. In giving birth, a woman can identify with how much her baby depends on her because she is connected to feelings in herself that go back to the time when she experienced that same dependence herself. And while she may feel great joy and satisfaction in responding to her baby's needs, a part of her is also likely to be crying out for someone to understand her own fears and anxieties and her need to be cared for.

Through childbirth, a woman gets in touch with deeper feelings in herself which she cannot always share with her partner because he finds it harder to accept similar feelings in himself. She feels she has been profoundly changed by the experience and that she has grown emotionally in a way her husband does not appear to want to recognize and understand. Yet while she cares for her baby, a woman has a great need for her husband's understanding as she is so dependent on him for support. Being out of touch with each other's feelings at this most vulnerable time can make her feel isolated and resentful.

What a woman may not appreciate is the conflict her husband is also going through about becoming a father. However much love and pride he has for his child, he is also likely to feel some envy and resentment towards the baby for the changes it has brought in his marriage. How well he is able to accept and cope with feeling excluded from the powerful bonding between a mother and her child will depend on how much he was affected by similar feelings in his own childhood, such as when he felt he had 'lost' his own mother when younger brothers or sisters were born.

Before a baby arrives, every parent has a fantasy – an expectation – of what being a parent will be like. They may know that they are not going to be perfect parents, but what is harder to imagine is that as well as loving their child, they will also feel anger, resentment and envy towards it. They will have the same conflicting feelings towards their children as they had towards their own parents. Their ability to cope with their mixed feelings about parenthood depends to a large extent on how much they were able to overcome similar feelings in past relationships.

A woman is more likely to confront her own inner conflicts about motherhood because of her closeness to her baby at the beginning of its life. Whereas it is easier for her husband to escape disturbing feelings about being a father by plunging into his everyday working life. If he feels resentful and envious about being an outsider in the relationship between his wife and their child, he may try to restore his self-esteem and sense of belonging by immersing himself in his work or even in a relationship with someone else.

Without understanding each other's different feelings, a pattern can develop in the marriage where the husband always finds a way of escaping conflicts in his family life, while the wife continues to feel that she has been left to cope on her own. A wife can continue to make her husband feel excluded from the relationship she has with their child to punish him for not understanding how much she needed him after the baby was born.

When a couple become parents, their most vulnerable feelings come to the surface. Inwardly, they feel frightened and over-whelmed by the grown-up responsibility they have taken on, while at the same time they can feel almost as dependent on each other as their baby does on them. Their relationship is going through a transition – a time of change. By sharing their fears as well as their joy in becoming parents, they can strengthen their marriage and become closer to each other and to their child.

Until their first child was born, married life to Sheila and Jim hadn't seemed much different from being single. They had lived together for a year before their marriage and had always considered themselves good friends, as well as lovers. They shared an interest in each other's work, liked doing the same things and generally got on with each other.

There was a fundamental change in their relationship after their baby was born which neither of them had been prepared for. When Sheila held her newborn son she was amazed how vulnerable she felt. It was almost unbearable to imagine ever losing him. For the first time in their relationship, she also felt completely dependent on her husband. She had never seriously considered her marriage failing before, but now she realized how scared she was that something would go wrong and that Jim would leave her.

Both Sheila and Jim had agreed that she should give up her teaching job for at least a year after the baby was born, so she could concentrate on being a mother. Motherhood was an experience that Sheila had expected to be completely satisfy-ing, so it came as a shock when it did not altogether live up to her expectations. However much she enjoyed being with her baby, there were times when she felt trapped and isolated. Being a mother was so emotionally consuming that she often felt she had lost touch with the person she was before her son was born. What Sheila had not recognized was how much she had depended on her job to give her a sense of identity. Having her own career had made her feel an equal partner in her marriage. It had also given her a sense of independence, so she had never fully realized how emotionally dependent she had always been on her husband.

Sheila was so afraid of feeling dependent on Jim that she resented what appeared to be his independence. He was the one who had a job which gave him financial security and a separate identity. He could walk out on her, whereas she depended on him providing for her and the baby, which made her feel intensely vulnerable to him and his moods.

When Jim came home, he seemed caught up in what had gone on at work, while all she had got to talk about was little incidents that had happened with the baby. She was acutely aware of him switching off from her or seeming bored because she found herself needing to chatter after being by herself. Sheila felt motherhood had changed her from being a stimulating, lively companion into a clinging, demanding wife. Yet she was also angry with Jim for not understanding how much she needed him. She couldn't tell him how vulnerable she felt and how much she wanted his reassurance.

Jim was struggling with his own feelings. He had expected to be a good father, but watching Sheila give birth to their son had been a traumatic experience for him. At one stage, he had even hated this unseen child who was giving its mother so much pain, and those feelings had really disturbed him. He had changed nappies, bathed the baby and generally done his bit as an involved father, but he knew it was Sheila, not him, that their tiny baby needed most. Seeing the bond between Sheila and their baby filled him with tenderness and love towards both of them. Yet it also made him feel shut out from their relationship and he was shocked by how envious and resentful he could feel when his wife seemed completely absorbed in their child. Jim also sensed that Sheila wanted more from him than he was giving, which only increased his guilt. He wanted to ask her what was wrong, but it felt as if she had shut herself off from him.

Jim felt more himself when he got to work. At least he knew what was expected of him there. He even found himself being more aware of the attractive young secretaries who worked in his office. They seemed flattered when he paid them attention and they took trouble to look nicely dressed, unlike Sheila who seemed to have lost interest in her own appearance.

After the baby arrived, love-making between Sheila and Jim became a rare occurrence. At first, Sheila's tiredness made it understandable, but gradually tiredness became more of an excuse. Sheila felt too resentful of her dependence on her husband to allow herself to feel vulnerable to him when they made love. Without realizing it, she had withdrawn emotionally and sexually from Jim to punish him for not understanding how needy she felt.

Sheila and Jim had made an outward commitment to each other when they took their marriage vows. But, inwardly, they had avoided feeling really committed to each other until they had had a child. Then they were forced to face their fears about being tied to each other in a 'till death do us part' relationship. They were no longer playing at being married. In having a baby, they had taken on a shared responsibility. They had reached a transition point through which their relationship needed to grow up. Sheila and Jim already had established a strong bond between them. Their ability to share similar interests and enjoy each other's company needed to be revived in their marriage. What they also needed was the courage to share the deeper and more conflicting feelings that they had discovered in themselves through having a child. Then a basically good relationship would become a rewarding, life-long partnership.

Some questions

- Are you grown up enough for marriage? Ask yourself the following questions:

  > Do you depend on having a partner to make you feel good about yourself and enable you to enjoy life?
  > Do you lose your sense of identity if you are not in a relationship?
  > Do you feel you need to live up to your parents' expectations by marrying the 'right' man?
  > Do you expect to be swept off your feet by Mr Right with whom you will live happily ever after?

  If the answer to these questions is Yes, you still have some growing up to do to achieve a fulfilling, lifetime partnership.

If you are married, here are some questions to think about that could help you to achieve a more mature and rewarding partnership.

- Has your marriage lived up to your expectations? If not, have you been able to accept and appreciate the ways in which your marriage is different from your fantasies about being a wife? Or are you feeling let down and disappointed because your dream did not turn into reality?

- How similar is your marriage to your parents? Are you able to incorporate good aspects of former important relationships in your life into your marriage? Or are you repeating old, negative relationship patterns that need to be discarded if your marriage is to develop into a more fulfilling partnership?

- Do you feel you have a sense of identity that does not depend on being a wife or a mother? Or have you lost touch with your own individuality by putting your family first and hiding your real self behind the roles you play in your marriage?

- Have you and your partner achieved an interdependence – a mutual partnership where you both depend on each other and also appreciate and enjoy each other's separate identities? Or do you feel threatened when your husband has different interests or ideas from you – or expects you to take up challenges in your own life and stand on your own feet without always relying on him to be the assertive, risk-taking partner?

- Has your marriage settled into a safe, familiar pattern – or are you prepared to face challenge and change in your relationship?

  Do you tend to blame your husband when you feel dissatisfied or frustrated – or are you able to see what it is within yourself that is stopping you achieving the satisfaction and fulfilment you want out of life?

- Are you prepared to struggle to understand yourself and your partner so your marriage continues to grow up into a truly rewarding partnership?

- Imagine losing your husband. Then begin to improve and appreciate what you have got in your marriage. No relationship lasts for ever!

7
Awakenings

This book began with an awakening of a princess who had been asleep for a long time. Hopefully, reading the book and answering the questions at the end of the chapters has also felt like an awakening because it has helped you understand yourself better and how you relate to your partner in a different way. That's all very well, you may say. But how can self-knowledge improve my relationship if my partner is not interested or willing to try and understand his own feelings, let alone mine?

A relationship can have more potential for change than we realize. When a woman becomes more self-aware, her attitude towards her partner changes. Instead of feeling overwhelmed and trapped in her own emotional conflicts, she has enough inner space to think her problems through. Instead of constantly reacting to her partner's moods or attitudes, she can give herself time to try and work out what is causing conflict between them, so she can talk to her partner about it in a more constructive way.

When our most vulnerable feelings are attacked, we often behave childishly because we are repeating childhood conflicts that still have the power to hurt us. But if we can develop enough self-awareness to be able to detach ourselves from the conflict, stand outside ourselves, so to speak, and look at what is happening, we develop a more grown-up ability to understand and sort out problems in our relationships and our lives. We are also more able to listen and try to understand our partner's feelings, even when they make us angry or cause pain.

By changing our attitude towards our partner, he is also likely to change. Instead of becoming defensive or withdrawing emotionally, he begins to feel more trusting and willing to listen to how we feel because his own feelings are being heard.

Couples can get locked into a pattern of relating that only brings out the worst in each other. But if a woman can detach herself from her relationship, stand back and look at what past conflicts are being repeated in her present-day life, she has begun to break the vicious circle of blame and guilt that she and her partner are caught in. Her attitude towards both herself and her partner becomes more understanding, accepting and loving. She is in touch with the more positive aspects of her personality, which allows her partner to respond with the positive elements within himself. They have started to bring out the best in each other, instead of the worst.

Judy, 28, and her partner Tim met through working in the same office. When they first started dating, Judy's position as sales manager in the firm was senior to Tim's, who was a sales rep.

Tim was very ambitious and Judy was aware of his underlying resentment of her being more successful than him. He tried to make a joke to their friends about going out with the boss, but she knew that he hated feeling in an inferior position. Tim was always complaining about the difficulties of working in the same office as the person he was having a relationship with. So finally Judy got the message and found herself a similar job with another firm, leaving her position as sales manager vacant for Tim to step into.

At first, it seemed like the perfect solution. But Judy's new job did not turn out to be as interesting as the one she had given up for Tim. Whereas Tim threw himself into his first executive position with such drive and enthusiasm that very soon he was being given additional responsibilities and a higher salary than Judy had earned.

Judy and Tim began to argue constantly. She accused him of being over-ambitious and selfish, always putting work before her. Tim's unrecognized guilt about pressuring Judy to leave the job he had now stepped into, and his need to prove he could do it better than her, made him feel angry and resentful.

Judy and Tim's competitiveness and their envy of each other's success prevented them from taking pride in their separate achievements. So much underlying resentment had built up between them that they could no longer see their positive qualities which had also attracted them to each other. Once they had realized how much their relationship had been affected by them becoming rivals, not partners, they became more aware of their competitiveness towards each other and were able to prevent it from continuing to have such a damaging effect. When they both stopped wanting to see the worst in each other, they were able to use their relationship to bring out the best in both of them.

Sleeping Beauty's sleep can be looked at in two ways. It can appear that all the princess had to do was wait passively for the right man to find her, which is a fantasy many women hang onto all their lives.

Sleep, in psychological terms, also represents being in touch with unconscious processes, which need to undergo change if we are to have different and more rewarding relationships than the ones we have previously experienced. Looked at in that way, Sleeping Beauty was in touch with the inner changes in herself, which is what enabled her prince to find her.

Our outer experiences are reflections of our inner world. When life seems chaotic and disorganized, what is being reflected is a chaotic and disordered inner state of mind. We may say that we consciously do things in our external lives to achieve a peaceful, calm state of mind. But we have already reached an inner state where our need for peace and calm outweighs more conflicting feelings, and it is that need we express in our outer activities and pursuits. Similarly, the kind of relationships we have reflect our inner needs. Just waiting for the right man to come along and show us how to have a mature, fulfilling relationship, not only won't happen but is looking at ourselves the wrong way round. We are waiting for something external to happen, without realizing that we have to go through a process of inner change first if we are to achieve the kind of relationship we want.

Inner change happens without us being aware of it. We can often see how we have changed if we look back on relationships we once had and realize that we have grown out of the need for those kind of experiences. We can see that we look for different qualities in a partner than we did when we were younger because we have changed inwardly through our experiences in life.

The more self-aware we become, the more likely we are to attract and be attracted to a partner who has the emotional maturity that we have been looking for. We are drawn to someone who values us for our real selves, not our looks or our ability to charm and seduce.

Relationships give meaning to our lives. Our 'other half' is what a partner is often called. A woman recognizes an otherness in a man, just as she recognizes the masculine qualities her father possessed as different from her own when she was a very small child. That otherness in our partner reflects another side of our own psychological make-up. Aspects of our lover are also ones we need to become aware of in ourselves. When that happens, it is as if we have found the 'other half' of ourselves, which makes us feel whole.

That is not to say that life becomes meaningless without a close, personal relationship. A woman can discover this other side of her nature in her relationship to her career and in any pursuit that challenges her and brings out the more forceful, adventurous side of her personality. But while she needs to discover her masculine aspects to bring out the best in herself, she also needs to stay firmly in touch with her essential femininity. If she lets her masculine qualities dominate the rest of her personality, she becomes a parody of real masculinity, a domineering, bossy woman, the sort who always wants to wear the trousers.

It is creating a balance between these two aspects of her nature that give a woman a sense of wholeness. A man and a woman also need to struggle to achieve a balance between the different masculine and feminine aspects in their personalities to create a feeling of wholeness in their relationship.

Balance is a key word. We are always striving to achieve balance in all sorts of ways in our lives. At the same time, we are also inwardly struggling to achieve a balance between opposing forces in our own nature.

The greatest challenge in a relationship is to achieve an interdependence which is based on two apparently conflicting aims: to be dependent on someone else, and to retain one's own independence and individuality.

We search for meaning in our lives and we come up with many different answers. The outer search for meaning reflects the inner struggle of being able to express our own individuality. Then whatever we do in life has meaning because it becomes an outward expression of our real selves. Putting our whole selves into whatever experience life offers is what helps us mature into the kind of woman who knows who she is, what she wants from her life and who she wants to share it with. If we feel life only has meaning if we have a partner, we deny ourselves the ability to get to know ourselves as individuals. If we always need to be dependent on someone else, we can never really feel a person in our own right. Being alone and feeling unloved stirs up all sorts of hidden fears. But without coming to terms with those anxieties within ourselves and developing our ability to be alone, we limit ourselves by our need always to cling to others.

The independent woman faces the reverse problems in a relationship. When she falls in love, the strength of her feelings towards her partner makes her feel dependent on him. She is in touch with her vulnerability, which she may have protected herself from by her independent lifestyle. The challenge for her is to balance these opposing needs in herself, so she can master her fears about real intimacy.

As I have tried to show in this book, the path towards self-knowledge leads back to childhood. What happened to us in the past is still indelibly printed on our present-day experiences. It goes back even further. If you look at the psychological history of a family's relationships over several generations, you can see the same pattern of relating being handed down from parents to their children. The chances are that the emotional difficulties that we have are similar to those our parents passed on to us because they had remained unresolved problems from their own backgrounds.

The way that we can break the pattern and bring about change, both in our lives and in our children's, is to become aware of these destructive elements in our personalities that cause such problems in our relationships. By understanding why we have needed to protect ourselves in such negative ways in our relationships, we get in touch with our real feelings and begin to understand ourselves better. We realize how our exaggerated childhood fears of anger, hurt, humiliation, rejection and loss have continued to haunt us throughout our adult years, so that we have limited both our enjoyment of life and our ability to experience our relationships in a fuller and more meaningful way.

We have become real-life Sleeping Beauties, sleeping our lives away.

Awakening is not easy. Choosing to face reality rather than staying asleep in fairy-tale fantasies of living happily ever after if only we meet the right man, is a similar transition to the letting go of childhood and facing the challenge of adult life. The paradox is that once we do that, we discover the child within us in a much more real way than when we were 'asleep'. That's because we rediscover our liveliness and our spontaneity which exists within our most intense and vulnerable feelings.

The thorn bushes that surrounded Sleeping Beauty's castle are the same as the protections that we surround ourselves with to prevent anyone getting too close to us. But once we no longer need that protection, we are more open to what life has to offer us. We are able to recognize a kiss from a real-life prince because we have awakened our real selves.